The Primacy of Ethics

Dag G. Aasland

Preface

This book is an elaborated translation of a Norwegian book (Aasland 2017). The elaboration is partly due to the transfer from a Norwegian to an international context, partly to new ideas, new knowledge and events that have come about in the last six years.

The work on the book has taken place in meetings with people and knowledge. Some of these meetings have been planned, others have not. The most difficult thing has not been choosing what to include, but rather what not to include, so that the message in the book is not drowned in an unnecessary number of words.

When adequate knowledge is to be obtained from several areas, it is absolutely necessary to get good help from others. I would first like to thank my workplace, University of Agder, which has facilitated, and drawn me into, many formative and fruitful learning processes together with students, colleagues and external partners. I would also like to thank them for the opportunity I had to be part of the management of a new and small but rapidly growing university. It has taught me a lot about reality outside of my comfort zone. Next, I would like to thank my editor, Ellen Aspelund at Gyldendal Academic Publishers for the good balance between encouragement and challenges. Through her, I also received good help from two skilled professional consultants: Lars Smith, who helped me with knowledge about the early development of the brain and the psychology of the smallest children, and Magdalene Thomassen, who has given me both professional philosophical support and a reality orientation towards the welfare professions, as well as a valuable academic criticism that has helped make the book better than it would have been otherwise. Thanks also to the Norwegian publisher for permission to publish the book in English.

I will thank MayFly Books and its editorial team, for me represented by Steffen Boehm, Toni Ruuska and Charles Barthold, for their willingness to publish and for their challenges to the draft that have led to a better English version.

Finally, but definitely most, I would like to thank my dear wife Helga Aasland, who started it all by putting me on the trail of the new knowledge about brain development in infants and the importance of early interaction for the further development of humans. And of course for all the support, encouragement and belief in the project along the way, not least through the daily stories about what it's like to be a professional helper today.

Grimstad, Norway, October 2023

Contents

Introduction

To understand how ethics work in today's society, professional help is a good place to start. By professional help, we primarily mean those who work in the health and social care sector and in elderly care. In addition, there are those who help children, in nurseries and in schools.

The characteristic of these professions is that ethics form a basis both in professional knowledge and in daily work. The criterion for what is relevant knowledge for these professions is the extent to which it is helpful to the other person, i.e. the person in need of help. This ethics is not just something that is learned through an education. It is an ethic which, together with an energy and a motivation, is retrieved from something that lies deeper in the body and mind than what an education alone can add. It is this underlying ethics that this book will try to illuminate.

But what if we go to the other end of the scale, to professions and businesses that are explicitly driven by the actors' self-interest? This is precisely what is considered to be the most important driving force in a market economy. Here, the criteria for what is relevant knowledge are how well it serves one's own and one's company's interests, and not how well it helps others. In business, ethics therefore often comes in as a demand from the outside, from society, when someone feels that the pursuit of self-interest has gone too far and too much at the expense of the community. In order to be able to handle this challenge from the outside, business has developed its own knowledge called business ethics, or corporate social responsibility.

But ethics in business has not only emerged as a response to society's reactions. It also has a more internal origin. In the business world, we find people who are genuinely interested in helping their customers. When a market economy is in many places possible to live with, and to live in, despite the fact that self-interest is a driving force, it is because it is populated by humans who, like most humans, generally behave decently towards each other.

In light of this, we can say that in all people, regardless of whether they work primarily for others or they work primarily for themselves and their own business, there is an ethic that does not always rise to the surface of consciousness, language and professional knowledge. In other words, there is an ethics at the bottom of and between all people. It is precisely this ethics that I want to explore in more detail in this book.

An important motivation for writing this book has been that during the last generation (or, to be more precise, the last 30–35 years) a lot of new knowledge has been gained about the brain, and in particular the early development of the brain, the first two years after birth. This is a knowledge that brings us an important step closer to understanding what has by some been called "the missing link" between biological reality and the world of ideas, between the concrete world of experience we live in and our abstract understanding of it, or, if one wants, between the objective and the subjective. This new knowledge points to the fact that such dichotomies can in themselves stand in the way of new insight, because it creates a blind spot that covers the very area where the two worlds meet. As I came across this knowledge, my thoughts gradually began to gather around the following questions: Shouldn't this new knowledge about how the brain develops, and especially about how consciousness and language arise in the biological organism, by means of an early interaction with a caregiver, change much of how we view the relationship between words and reality? And further: Does this knowledge not contain the possibility of a new, and perhaps more concrete and realistic approach to what we think about what is good and right, both for others and for ourselves? This book has been written in the hope of finding out more about these questions.

We humans live in the physical world, and in this world we have developed an ability to communicate, both with and without the use of words. But while this physical world is continuous in time and space, the world of words can only consist of separate entities, even when words are put together in sentences and longer explanations. This means that physical proximity enables communication and interaction that can never be replaced by words. It also means that a helper who is physically present with the person to be helped has an advantage that others, such as a manager, who primarily communicates with words, do not have. This is an advantage that is easily neglected, consciously or not, partly because it is beyond a manager's control. At the same time, it is precisely in this common, close physical world that both knowledge and ethics have their source. But what does that really mean?

We will always have to relate to an objectively given reality, but there is not one and only one objectively correct way to describe this reality. We will never get there, for reasons that I will get more into later. What is an objectively given fact, however, is that thinking and feeling can be registered as neurobiological processes in the body, while both thinking and feeling are experienced subjectively. There is still much we don't know about this, but we at least know enough to be able to say that even though thought and action models are presented as rational and consistent systems, they are created in a physical context that is far more real than ideas like rationality and consistency. It applies to models for goal and result management, and it applies to scientific models that are supposed to explain what happens in a body, in nature, in a human mind and in a society. We will never be able to fully understand this reality, precisely because the tool we have to understand it with is the same consciousness that is part of, and in a way only forms the surface of, these processes.

A book about the primacy of ethics, starting with exploring what we can learn from the daily life of professional helpers, must necessarily put rational theories in context with a not always equal rational practice. The world we live in today can in many ways be called rationalistic, in the sense that rationality, i.e. logically consistent thinking, free of internal contradictions, is held up as a norm and an ideal for thoughts and actions, especially in working life. At the same time, we do not have to look around much to be able to confirm that the world is not at all rational in this sense. Seen from the inside of an organisation, there may rather be reason to ask whether people are to a greater extent governed by their emotions. Perhaps we are actually governed by the need and desire for a meaning, or to be able to see what we do and what we are in a larger context? These questions have led me to the 17th-century philosopher Baruch Spinoza, who offers an alternative to his more famous colleague from the generation before him, René Descartes, who in turn became a founder of modern science, with his prescriptions for methodical and systematic thinking. In retrospect, we can say that Spinoza has not managed to shake the hegemony that Descartes has had in our thinking until today. The knowledge we have gained in recent years about how people's reason is connected to their emotions, and how these can now be observed and increasingly understood as bodily processes, makes Spinoza more relevant, and Descartes perhaps correspondingly less so.

It is not difficult to see that in scientifically based education for many of the helping professions there is a strikingly asymmetrical relationship between the genders. While the students often have a majority of women, the knowledge they are set to acquire, especially the knowledge from previous generations, is often collected and written down by men. There may of course be nothing wrong with this in the first place, but there is still a risk that the renewal of the knowledge that women can contribute by drawing on their experiences and perspectives, can be delayed. All the chapters in this book are based on important sources of knowledge from previous generations, all of whom are men. Each chapter then develops these men's work by adding new knowledge, and, in an attempt to make a small contribution to the necessary renewal, each chapter ends with a woman's voice, either as a corrective, as a supplement, or in a dialogue with the established knowledge. What these women have in common is that they have a story to tell. I will return more to how the narrative can come before any theory, and that it even makes sense to say that the narrative comes before thinking.

All the chapters have been written based on the recognition that we as thinking, acting and helping humans are always parts of a larger context. The chapters are also connected, in a train of thought. The first chapter shows how conscious thinking occurs in the organism, in an interaction with another human being, so that we can communicate with each other, but also so that we can develop into more or less independent individuals. The second chapter elaborates on this by showing how the narratives keep us together, while our attempts at what we call rational thinking in many ways separate us from each other, and at times set us up against each other. This is further elaborated in the third chapter, which attempts to show how the words, even those used in a scientifically produced knowledge, are vanishingly small individual parts in an infinitely larger reality. The fourth chapter deals with what we see as a good and right action, which cannot be captured by words, but instead is often about finding a way back to something that existed before any words. In the fifth chapter, I try to gather everything into a larger whole, with good help from Spinoza, but also with help from the women we have met along the way. Finally, the book will close with a concluding remark on business, ethics and the future, suggesting that the origin of ethics is interpersonal rather than external, an assumption that also is best suited for our common efforts towards a sustainable development.

Chapter 1:
The thinking human

The life behind thoughts

When biologists were once going to find a Latin name on us humans as a species, where evolution has brought us, and which should distinguish us from the other species, they chose the name *Homo sapiens*, which means the thinking human. No other animal could, as far as it was possible to register, think, and at least not use this thinking, in the same way as humans.

But isn't thinking only partially adequate as a description of what it is to be human? What about our capacity for compassion? What about our spontaneous impulses to help others, also outside our own kin, before any thoughts are thought? Here, an expert will answer that it depends on what we mean by thinking. Or perhaps more precisely: Here it will depend on what kind of expert we ask. As indicated in the introduction, thinking means at least two different things: on the one hand, the neurobiological processes that can be observed by scanning a brain and, on the other hand, the subjective experience of thinking, which leads to what we call thoughts, and which we can express in words, either orally or in writing. And the first meaning of thinking encompasses more than the second meaning: Not all thinking in the first meaning reaches consciousness and is put into words. On the other hand, such measurable neurobiological processes are not at all reserved for humans. In other words, there is a need for further clarifications.

The two aforementioned meanings of thinking must in any case have something to do with each other. There must be a connection between an observable activity in the brain and how this activity is eventually expressed, by the owner of the brain, in words. This chapter will be about what we know of this connection.

In today's society, it is debated whether there is a danger that robots and other computer-controlled tools can make humans redundant. As long as people in working life are expected to only use their ability to act based on written instructions, and preferably not use other sides of themselves, sides that we otherwise associate with "the humane", such as helping someone as a spontaneous action, it is easy to understand the reason for this concern. Ever since the breakthrough of industrial societies, the machine has in many ways been held up as an ideal for human participation in working life. This ideal has been carried further to a significant extent in the post-industrial service society. We can easily get the impression that a good employee is one who does the tasks he or she is assigned to, tasks which should preferably be described in as much detail as possible in instructions, agreements and job descriptions, and which should later be reported. When such tasks have not yet been replaced by machines, it is mostly because the technology and the knowledge needed to program a machine have not advanced far enough. But as computer technology becomes increasingly advanced, the more such tasks can be taken over by machines.

But then we may ask: What about all the other sides of being human? What about our ability to empathize and care for others, or the ability to deviate from a pre-planned plan, which in some cases may involve a risk, but which can also lead to new and better ways of performing a task? Perhaps these human abilities are more important than we realize? Perhaps there are some advantages to the fact that the tasks that a machine can perform are actually left to machines, so that people no longer have to experience themselves as machines, but instead can do what machines cannot do? Wouldn't that make jobs more meaningful? In that case, it will require a different way of looking at labour, not just for some, such as those who already have what we can call creative professions, but for everyone, including those who work directly and concretely with production and service provision.

We see today that many people fall outside organized working life, and it often starts with them falling outside already at school. Perhaps part of the problem lies in the fact that working life – and schools – are too directed towards what can be put into words, and too little recognizes the value of all the other sides of the human, where abilities can be distributed completely differently, and perhaps a bit out of control for a manager – or teacher? If we had been more aware of these other aspects, perhaps it would also have given us a more humane society?

The rest of this chapter will present some of what we know today about the connection between what happens in us unconsciously and what reaches consciousness and which we put into words. We will take a closer look at knowledge that has been gained over the past 30–35 years, about how the brain develops in the period shortly after birth. This knowledge challenges the traditional distinction between natural sciences and human sciences. In order to be able to put this knowledge into context, we shall go back to one who was active hundred years ago, and who laid a good foundation for our understanding of what happens "behind the thoughts", namely Sigmund Freud, the man who discovered the importance of the unconscious.

Freud's discovery

Sigmund Freud was born in 1856 in the town of Freiberg in what was then Austria-Hungary. Today, the city is called Příbor and is located in the Czech Republic. As a newly qualified medical doctor, he would most like to go into anatomical studies of the brain, to find out how the various areas of the brain work, and how they act on us, and for us, as humans. But that was not an interest he could make a living from. Freud wanted to marry and eventually start a family, and then he needed a steady income. Therefore, he instead opened a private medical practice in Vienna, where he received patients from the city's wealthy bourgeoisie. In order to get as close as possible to his main interest, neurology, he received patients who struggled with mental health (Matthis 2014: 272).

Freud listened to the patients' stories in order to try to understand what their world of thought was like, and to find out whether in their life stories there could be a key to their problems and thus also to a way out of the problems. He found this so interesting that it became his specialty. Thus, psychoanalysis was established, as a new approach to and understanding of the human mind.

With his education as a medical doctor, Freud probably felt an affinity with the natural sciences for a long time. In any case, he embarked on an ambitious project to turn psychology into a natural science: "Project for a scientific psychology" (Freud 1966). But after much effort, he finally gave up on this project. As psychoanalysis developed, he realized that a purely objective, scientific perspective on the human mind can only provide a limited knowledge. This was an important discovery for Freud himself, but it was even more important for science. In the introduction to Freud's aborted "Project for a Scientific Psychology", published in 1950, i.e. long after his death in 1939, and republished in his collected works in English, the editor, James Strachey, who has also translated Freud's own text into English, is quite clear:

> "...we must remember that Freud himself ultimately threw over the whole neurological framework. Nor is it hard to guess why. For he found that his neuronal machinery had no means of accounting for what, in *The Ego and the Id*, he described as being 'in the last resort our one beacon-light in the darkness of 'depth-psychology' – namely, the property of being conscious or not'. In his last work, the posthumous *Outline of Psycho-Analysis*, he declared that the starting-point of the investigation into the structure of the psychical apparatus 'is provided by a

fact without parallel, which defies all explanation or description – the fact of consciousness', and he adds this footnote: 'One extreme line of thought, exemplified in the American doctrine of behaviorism, thinks it possible to construct a psychology which disregards this fundamental fact!' It would be perverse indeed to seek to impute a similar disregard to Freud himself. The *Project* must remain a torso, disavowed by its own creator." (Strachey 1966: 293).

The later in Freud's writings we come, the clearer it becomes to us that he has transcended the objective, natural scientific approach, simply because through his experience with patients and his desire to help them he realized that it is also important to understand how patients put their own subjective experiences into words. The objective and the subjective perspective are therefore not opposed to each other, it is rather the case that they complement each other and must be put together in order to obtain the best possible knowledge that can be in the patient's best interest.

Through his practice, Freud became more and more interested in what he called the unconscious, and which he imagined as a kind of separate world inside the human mind, behind the conscious thought. He came to the conclusion that the mind must in a way interchange between the conscious and the unconscious. In other words, a thought was not lost because it was not conscious. It could appear again at a later time (Freud 1957).

Before we leave Freud to look at more recent knowledge that has corrected and supplemented him, we shall consider one more of his central concepts, the further development of which we shall see later. It is the term called *id* (in German *das Es*). In the little book *The Ego and the Id*, which was referred to in the quotation above, we can read how he tries to summarize his experiences from the many meetings with patients and the discussions with colleagues.

Firstly, Freud, as I have already mentioned, makes a distinction between the conscious and the unconscious, where "consciousness is the *surface* of the mental apparatus" (Freud 1961: 19). So, when he tries to describe the ego as a subject, which has its consciousness, he realizes that in this ego-subject, there is also something of the unconscious. I am not always aware of what I am doing. But at the same time, Freud believes that a large part of the unconscious lies outside the ego, a place we can imagine lies deeper in the unconscious. It is something that I, as a subject, cannot call forth, but which has a kind of will of its own. This is what he calls *id*. It is not only outside the ego's control, Freud also came to the conclusion that it in many ways controls the ego:

> "The functional importance of the ego is manifested in the fact that normally control over the approaches to motility devolves upon it. Thus in its relation to the id it is like a man on horseback, who has to hold in check the superior strength of the horse; with the difference, that the rider tries to do so with his own strength while the ego uses borrowed forces. The analogy may be carried a little further. Often a rider, if he is not to be parted from his horse, is obliged to guide it where it wants to go; so in the same way the ego is in the habit of transforming the id's will into action as if it were its own." (Freud 1961: 25).

Later in his book, Freud introduces the "superego", as an ideal ego, a vestige of parental authority, which helps the ego to limit the *id*'s control over the ego.

This *id*—which lies deep in our minds, usually inaccessible to our consciousness, but nevertheless as something determining our thoughts—we shall meet again later from other knowledge. Later in this chapter and in later chapters we will see it as neurobiological processes, but now as supplementary knowledge to a subjective experience of consciousness, as Freud also realized the importance of. In chapter 4, we will see how the French philosopher Emmanuel Levinas tries to describe how ethics arises in the encounter with the face of the Other, which evokes in me something that is "prior to all memory and all recall" (page 65).

Freud's insight has been fundamental to the further development of knowledge about the human mind. But at the same time, his texts are also expressions of what was possible to know in his time. Today we have many of the opportunities to study what happens in the brain, which Freud did not have. Today, we can also combine this knowledge with the subjective knowledge that a person can account for from his own world of thought. We will now take a closer look at this.

Newer knowledge about the development of the brain

Freud thus did not get as far as he would have liked in his attempts to connect psychoanalysis with brain research. But those who later carried Freud's theories and practice forward, and who have developed the knowledge to what it is today, have come a long way on this path. Today we have knowledge about how the brain develops from birth, a knowledge that has proven to be a good supplement to the knowledge that psychoanalysis can give us.[1]

Even before birth, the child naturally has a connection to the mother, which normally continues after birth. We can say that this connection is an emotional communication. Words such as "emotional" and "communication" are of course words that are added afterwards to what is already taking place, with the limitations that always lie in putting words to something real. It is not the words that decide what happens, it is rather what happens that creates our desire to put it into words.

Between the two bodies both before and after birth, and after birth also between the two faces, there is an interaction that constantly shapes the child's brain to function as evolution has given it the opportunity to. This shaping of the child's brain occurs partly as a thinning of redundant connections (synapses) between brain cells, partly as a connection of functional networks of brain cells.

---

1 The description that follows is partly taken from Schore (1994), especially chapter 35, "The Dialogical Self and the Emergence of Consciousness" (pp. 490–498). In addition, I would like to thank professor Lars Smith for important supplementary knowledge and for references to other literature in the area.

Those good moments with a face-to-face nonverbal communication between mother and child, accompanied by typical baby sounds can immediately seem quite ordinary, but in reality there is a lot going on. Through all the senses and communication channels, the new brain is here "set up", much like a new computer has to be set up when it comes straight from the factory.

This interaction happens completely unconsciously in the child, and also initially in the mother. An interesting insight into what happens in this interaction can be found in Lars Smith's elaboration of the term "intuitive care practice" (Smith 2014).

I suggested above that this early interaction between mother and child might be compared to what is done with a new computer. The machine must be "set up" by an operator, and this is done by connecting it to another computer with ready-made programs, so that the new machine will be able to enter the programs that the user may later wish to have. However, there are important differences between how a new brain is enabled to use its potential, and how a new computer is set up. I will go into these differences in more detail in a later chapter (chapter 3), but for now we can in any case say that what happens in and between brains and bodies happens continuously and not in discrete words or numbers, while what happens when a computer is set up, consists of several separate steps in a planned procedure. Another difference is that this interaction not only changes the child, but also the mother (Lewis 2014: xi-xii).

The necessary emotional communication that the child has first with the mother and gradually with other people is normally such that positive emotions are reinforced, such as by returning a smile with a smile, while negative emotions, such as pain or despair, are met with comfort and empathy. In the professional language, this is called affect regulation. Through this regulation, the child becomes increasingly more able to regulate not only its own emotions, but also how active it should be in the interaction. The child also needs to take breaks in the interaction, in order to have the opportunity to process information. Through normal affect regulation, the child's emotions are regulated so that they do not completely take over, which can lead to actions that can destroy both oneself and others.

The emergence of consciousness

Around the middle of the second year of life, the development of the new brain has progressed so far that the child begins to gain an awareness of itself. In the interaction with others, the child gradually begins to be able to distinguish between itself and the other. It imitates the other, it begins to be able to participate in a dialogue, first wordlessly and gradually with typical baby sounds, which eventually turn into words. The child experiences the joy and relief of being understood by others. The British neurophysiologist Horace Barlow (who, incidentally, is Darwin's great-grandson) has launched a hypothesis that consciousness is something evolution has developed over time so that we can survive through the advanced form of communication with each other that language represents. To think, in the sense of forming thoughts within oneself, is to communicate with oneself, which can be seen as a way of practicing communication with another, suggests Barlow (1980: 83). When we put this idea of consciousness as an "organ" of communication between people together with the quote from Freud above that the ego depends on the *id* in the same way that a rider depends on the horse, we can imagine a more modern picture: consciousness is not the head of the organism, but rather its "communication department". In the same way that the communication department of an organization does not control the organization, consciousness does not control the organism; rather, its function is to formulate the will of the organism in words, as if this will were rational, consistent, and reasonable. But the organism (or organization) behind the picture that consciousness (the communication department) draws, is in reality filled with lots of emotions, contradictions, non-conscious processes and partly chaos.

Conscious thinking is thus an ability we have developed through evolution, which makes communication and interaction with others more efficient. But it is still the case that the path from the emotional to the cognitive (thinking) does not happen in leaps and bounds, it happens as a continuous process, which can be followed as a neurobiological development.[2]

Based on this knowledge, we can therefore state that our thinking activity, in the sense of putting words to thoughts that are then used in speech and writing, is part of all the neurobiological processes that take place in the body. The emotions that arise are part of the same processes, but in addition there is everything that happens that is not available to us, as either thoughts or emotions. And to return to Freud's original ambitions: The knowledge that is revealed through a psychoanalysis, which is based on the patient's subjective experiences and own world of thought, and the knowledge that is revealed through neurological examinations, where the patient is an object for the person in charge of the examination, supplements each other in the efforts to gain an ever better understanding of what is happening in our minds (Matthis 2014). As in all other subject areas, we will constantly gain better knowledge here too, but we will never be able to get to the point where we can say that we now know everything. The reason for that is obvious in this particular case: Our only tool to acquire systematic and consistent knowledge is precisely the consciousness that we are exploring at the same time, and which we now know is only a small part of something much larger and only one of several sources of insight in a broader sense. The new knowledge therefore does not lead us to a belief that one day we can understand everything, quite the opposite. Rather, it makes us more humble, because we realize that our (that is, our consciousness') ability to understand ourselves is and will always be limited. This is a limitation inherent in the tool itself.

In retrospect, we can note that Freud's work here has been supplemented by neurobiological knowledge in a way that corresponds to his choice to abandon the "Project for a Scientific

---

2 This does not mean that this continuous development of the individual brain is a kind of repetition of evolution. Here we only look at the first-mentioned development of the brain and not at how evolution has brought us to the people we are today.

Psychology" (see above), which could have led to what he strongly warned against in "the American behaviourist doctrine". There can sometimes seem to be some strong professional contradictions between psychoanalysis on the one hand and a more behaviourist, or behavioural psychology, approach on the other. While the first takes a subjective point of departure, the second tries to adopt a more objective perspective. But eventually more and more professionals, whether they work theoretically or clinically, have realized that both perspectives can have something to offer. The knowledge that is created through observations of neurobiological processes and of behaviour becomes a supplement to the knowledge that is obtained with the help of the subjective consciousness, and vice versa. We thus have two different sources of a common knowledge, but which can never be combined into one, precisely because they have different starting points.

We read almost daily about new and exciting discoveries in brain research. But we more and more seldom meet the attitude among scientists that was perhaps more common in Freud's time, that we are now one step closer to the day when we can say that we know everything. It is rather the opposite: With increased knowledge about the brain also comes increased knowledge about the limitations of consciousness, and thus also about all that we can never know.

The limits of rationality

Despite—or perhaps rather because of—the humility that the discovery of the limitations of consciousness teaches us, this new knowledge opens some new and exciting doors in our attempts to orient ourselves in the world. What we call "knowledge" on a daily basis is that which can be described with the help of language, and which has as an overriding, regulating criterion to be in accordance with the reality it describes, and at the same time not contain any internal contradictions. But now we know that this knowledge is managed by a consciousness, which we are equipped with each one of us, and that this consciousness is really only a surface of something far more, namely all the neurobiological processes that take place in the body. Consciousness, emotions and, in addition, all the processes that we neither know nor feel (including what Freud, based on his assumptions, tentatively called *id*), are connected in a continuous set of processes.

It also means that there are other sources of knowledge, both about ourselves and about the world, than the word "knowledge" usually refers to. Art is an example of ways of communicating that do not belong to the usual concept of knowledge. When art works as art, it conveys something from one person to another. It creates a resonance with the recipient. We can say the same about other cultural expressions, such as stories and myths, where religion is also a part. This is also a form of knowledge about ourselves that is not part of the scientifically produced knowledge, but which comes in addition to this.

An example of this is the Bible's account of the Fall. Adam and Eve disobeyed God and ate from the tree of knowledge. Then they were expelled from Paradise, and for the first time they felt shame about not being covered (Gen 3, 7). Several researchers have concluded that the child's first awareness of itself (at around 18 months) begins with the experience of shame (Schore 1994: 493). The child discovers for the first time that it is being seen and evaluated by others, and thus that it is a separate subject, but who can therefore also engage in dialogue with another. Could it be that the mythology here makes sense to us because our body "remembers" something that our consciousness does not remember?

We are bodies that, even before we were born, have learned to communicate with other bodies. We can read each other's faces, we can empathize with each other, we can amplify each other's emotions, and, as an added bonus from evolution: We can also use words and thoughts in this communication. But everything is connected. There is a continuity between thoughts and emotions, and there is a continuity between these two and the "sea" of neurobiological processes that take place inside us all the time, but which do not reach our consciousness. There is also a connection between all this and what takes place in our physical surroundings. This is, in a way, self-evident, but we do not necessarily always take the consequences of it. If a social environment becomes too closed, be it political, religious or academic, a notion can spread that the most important thing is what happens in an abstract world of language and ideas, where the material, including our own body, and the nature around us is only necessary obstacles, or useful tools. It is easy for us to see ourselves and each other, also in working life, as heads without bodies that wander around and relate to each other only with words and concepts. Maybe it's time we put the head back on the body again?

Consequences for professional practice

Right from the beginning of the 20th century until today, working life has been organized based on a strong belief in the self-sufficiency of human rationality. An impressive development of new technology has led, and still leads, to great material progress. It has also influenced how we organize work, both in the private and public sector. Rational and unambiguous instructions and plans, goal management tools and quality assessment routines set the conditions for how a work should be carried out. On the professional side of the welfare state's professions, new "methods" are regularly launched with a strong appeal to our rationality (based on what is called evidence-based knowledge), which can seem enticing, both for the service practitioners themselves and for their managers, who have to keep the budgets. One of the reasons that makes these methods, and this knowledge, so appealing is that they can be understood and described explicitly in a logical system of thought and action. Moreover, they only build on what can be seen by everyone, and not on the professional's more hidden insight and personal experience integrated in the professional knowledge. In other words, they use only that part of human potential that can be put into words by the explicitly stated knowledge. Here we must again recall the two meanings of what it is to think. Forming thoughts in the form of words takes place on a surface in our minds, while what we mobilize when we help others, also professionally, are universal human functions that are embedded in the brain's deeper processes. That is, the extended meaning of thinking.

Today we know that the rational thinking and action systems used in working life are not closed, self-supporting systems. Both our thoughts and our actions have roots that extend further down in neurobiological processes, via the emotions to aspects of our personality and history that are not conscious to us. This insight is often ignored. In some places it is even an ideal to consciously put a lid on it, also in professions where the task is to help other people. If we ignore this additional source of knowledge, it is easy to react to other people's behaviour as if it were always guided by conscious thinking, and thus could be changed by changing this conscious thinking through instructions or other forms of direct regulation. In other words, as in programming a robot. Sometimes this can work, but it is probably because the rest of our mental potential, the non-rational, is mobilized in the same direction. By bringing out that in our potential as humans which is something more than being a robot, we can also ask ourselves to what extent the actions of others are an expression of emotions, for example fear or despair. Then our role as professionals can rather be to strengthen the affect regulation and the intuitive exercise of care that began (or should have begun) with the infant's mother, and with which we, with our ability to empathize, can help each other throughout our lives.

Action plans are a widespread tool in working life. The prerequisites behind an action plan are often that the way we carry out work is based exclusively—or at least mainly—on rational thinking. Or, at best, a prerequisite for an action plan to work is that the people who will carry out the tasks are also involved emotionally, and thus that the motivation also goes in the same direction. But by appealing exclusively to our ability to form rational thoughts, it can become difficult to use other sides of human potential, that is, what no machine can perform. We know that emotions mean a lot both between colleagues and in the relationships with those who receive our services. In a working life where technology is becoming increasingly advanced, it may become increasingly important to develop the ability to communicate emotionally, in addition to being able to communicate with a rational language. But it may be even more important to recognize that we can only know a vanishingly small part of what happens in a person, both in others and in ourselves. This realization will lie at the bottom of the rest of this book.

Consciousness cannot therefore be "complete". The limitation of our consciousness is one of the reasons why not all questions have an answer. We may see examples of this in the aftermath of terrorist actions where people have been killed. Especially during the following trials a discussion may rise about whether the perpetrator was sane or not. The judicial logic requires that this question has a correct answer that can be formulated in words. But maybe it doesn't? Perhaps the limitations of our brains to arrive at correct answers to any stated question mean that we are unable to answer some questions? Something similar can then also apply to less dramatic and more everyday cases, such as when it comes to making diagnoses or making plans.

Before we go any further with this, I want to present a woman who illustrates exactly what this chapter is about. Her approach is about acknowledging, and accepting, that there is something we will never know, also about what goes on inside ourselves.

Siri Hustvedt: The shaking woman

The American writer Siri Hustvedt tells in her book *The Shaking Woman or a History of my Nerves* (Hustvedt 2009) about her own experiences that she sometimes, but by no means all the times, suddenly begins to tremble while giving a speech. At the same time, the book conveys much of the knowledge that has been acquired in recent years, in the borderland between psychology and neurology. Here she also looks at science from the outside and adds knowledge to it from her own, subjective, perspective, both as an author and as a "patient", outside science's own boundaries.

Hustvedt has followed lectures in neurology and been invited to discussion groups in neuro-psychoanalysis, first at the New York Psychoanalytic Institute and then at Rockefeller University in New York. She is considered a pioneer in these frontier fields, someone who is used as a speaker in prestigious, international contexts (Øverland 2015).

In her book, we can read both about her unpleasant experiences with the tremors and about how she tried to find the cause of them, including by seeking professional help. She understood that it must have something to do with her relationship with her late father, Lloyd Hustvedt, who was a professor of Scandinavian literature at St. Olaf College in Minnesota. Perhaps there was something unclear in the relationship with him?

An ambitious psychoanalyst with an approach limited by scientific and rational knowledge would probably have tried "to get to the bottom of" this unresolved issue. Instead, Siri Hustvedt acknowledges, by expanding scientific knowledge with a subjective insight, that there is something that lies in an inaccessible memory in her body, and that she has to live with. It is thus something that she will never be able to gain full insight into, but which is just as fully and undoubtedly a part of herself and her nervous system, and thus also of her as a person, and which she has in any case become better acquainted with.

This is how Siri Hustvedt ends the book *The Shaking Woman or a History of my Nerves*:

> "Coherence cannot eliminate ambiguity... Ambiguity is not quite one thing, not quite the other. It won't fit into the pigeonhole, the neat box, the window frame, the encyclopedia. It is a formless object or feeling that can't be placed. Ambiguity asks, Where is the border between this and that?

Ambiguity does not obey logic. The logician says, "To tolerate contradiction is to be indifferent to truth." Those particular philosophers like to play games of true and false. It is one or the other, never both. But ambiguity is inherently contradictory and insoluble, a bewildering truth of fogs and mists and the unrecognizable figure or phantom or memory or dream that cannot be contained or held in my hands because it is always flying away, and I can't tell what it is or if it is anything at all. I chase it with words even though it won't be captured and, every once in a while, I imagine I have come close to it. In May 2006, I stood outside under a cloudless blue sky and started to speak about my father, who had been dead for over two years. As soon as I opened my mouth, I began to shake violently. I shook that day and then I shook again on other days. I am the shaking woman." (Hustvedt 2009: 198-199).

Chapter 2:
Words, words, words[3]

Introductory words

The previous chapter discussed how words are formed. This chapter will look at how they are used. We followed the path from one meaning of thinking to another: from the neurobiological processes that take place in the brain to the thoughts expressed in words. We saw that the child's self-awareness arises roughly in the middle of the second year of life in an interaction with another person, usually the mother, as a continuation of the emotional communication between the two. The ability to think is then developed in the sense of forming thoughts, with words, which can be seen as an exercise in communicating with an imagined other (Barlow 1980: 83). This happens in a continuous development. At the same time, we also saw in the previous chapter how Freud, through his experience with patients, discovered that the subjective perspective on one's own thoughts is also necessary in order to understand what happens in the human mind.

The use of words as expressions of thoughts, in their numerous combinations in sentences and further in larger written and oral explanations, is absolutely necessary for us; we depend on words in

---

3 "Words, words, words" was the answer Shakespeare's Hamlet gave when Polonius asked him "What do you read, my lord?"

almost everything we do. Especially in helping others, it is beyond any doubt that a sufficient supply of words, both with oneself and with the other, is absolutely necessary for us to be able to acquire knowledge and apply it.

But unfortunately there are examples of the words losing their hold in the world of reality. Abstract thought models can be communicated between people and can be made both impressively complex and captivatingly simple. Eventually, such thought models can live their own lives, as if they exist independently of human life and the material world. The result can sometimes be comical, like the beloved caricature of "the distracted and detached professor". At other times, such detached thought models can become downright dangerous, as when political or religious ideas take over the control of individual people's actions, perhaps precisely because they can be both impressively complex and captivatingly simple.

Skjervheim's warning

The Norwegian philosopher Hans Skjervheim (1926–1999) elegantly described how things can go wrong for those who lose themselves in the world of words, in an essay with the slightly intricate title "Invitation to (cultural(?)) suicide?" (Skjervheim 1992).

A recurring theme in Skjervheim's work is that the human sciences copy too much the methods of the natural sciences, by looking at people "from the outside", as objects. Thus, they overlook the fact that people are also subjects, and that their subjective understanding is an important part of knowledge about society and about humans.

In the previous chapter, we saw how Freud discovered through his practice that his scientific approach as a doctor was insufficient to understand the human mind. The patients' own stories about their lives and thoughts were important knowledge for Freud to be able to help them with their psychological problems. We saw that, as a result, he warned against turning psychology into a natural science, something he himself originally had great faith in, but which he eventually realized would only lead to what he warned against as "the

American doctrine of behaviourism" (page 11). A similar realization spread in Europe about the understanding of society, and it was precisely this insight that Skjervheim brought home to Norway from his studies of continental philosophy, especially from Germany.

Skjervheim grew up in a small community on the countryside in Western Norway. This background characterized his work, in that what we call "common sense" for him always trumped the pure and mutually consistent models of thought, which were the ideal in the natural sciences. When it comes to knowledge about society and man, he could quote an expression from his home place: "There isn't room for all knowledge in one head" (Sørbø 2002: 18).

In the aforementioned essay "Invitation to (cultural(?)) suicide?" Skjervheim uses common sense to criticize what is called postmodern thinking, which was particularly widespread in France in the 1970s and into the 1980s.[4] This is a way of thinking that calls into question whether the words we use actually refer to something real, a reality we like to think lies "behind" these words. We cannot know this for sure, the postmodern thinkers point out, language can be constructed independently of any underlying reality. The logical consequence of such a thought is that there is thus a great danger that the use of language becomes just a game of words, without any direct correspondence with an underlying reality. In his essay, Skjervheim suggests that the most important source of inspiration for these thoughts was the German philosopher Friedrich Nietzsche (1844–1900). Nietzsche had pointed out the problem that when we use language, we necessarily have to use the same word for real cases that are not identical. It is simply because the "number of real cases"—if that term can have any meaning at all—will always be too large to be covered by each individual word, no matter how many words we create. Thus, says Nietzsche, there is a gap somewhere already when people begin to think, the moment we take for granted that two identical cases exist in reality, because they are named with the same

---

4 Skjervheim mentions explicitly Michel Foucault, Jacques Derrida, Jean-François Lyotard og Gilles Deleuze.

word. This leads to people being misled from the very beginning. The conclusion that the postmodern thinkers draw from it, according to Skjervheim, is that all power is given to those who make us believe that two different cases are in reality the same because they are named with the same word. In that way, the rhetoric takes the inside swing of the factual argumentation, and there is no longer any difference between being convinced and being persuaded.

Skjervheim's response to this thinking is that he chooses not to go into it, because it undermines all science, including philosophy itself. What he believes is missing from the postmodern philosophers is the simple recognition that this weakness in using language that they point out is something that we simply have to live with, because we are completely dependent on language, as for instance in politics. Reality is thus more important than pure and rigorous logical thinking, and then we will have to set aside the rationalist philosophical ideals. Fortunately, people have what we call judgment to be able to do this. With our judgement, we can place ourselves "in life itself" and regard the purely philosophical thought exercises as precisely that: thought exercises. If we instead enter into these thought exercises, we risk being carried away by them. Then we can also risk getting lost in the logical wanderings as independently thinking subjects.[5]

Neurobiology's support to Skjervheim

Here, neurobiology comes in with an important additional knowledge that supports Skjervheim's scepticism of the postmodern philosophers. As we saw in the previous chapter, consciousness arises in a continuous process that begins with an emotional communication, first with the mother and then with other persons. The researchers who describe this say that the establishment of consciousness begins with mother and child creating stories together,

---

5 Skjervheim compared the postmodern philosophers he criticized to the Greek Empedocles, who, according to myth, jumped into the volcano Etna to explore it from the inside: He let himself be carried away in the service of science, but was lost as a thinking subject.

first without words—only with the universal baby sounds—and then with words. Narratives are important, these researchers say, because a narrative is something that binds one moment to the next and thus gives the child an experience of being a subject, who also "takes itself along" from one moment to the next, in the narrative (Schore 1994: 494–495).[6]

Here there is an interesting link to Nietzsche, as Skjervheim quotes him, when he points out the "lack" that occurs the moment a human begins to think, because different cases must be described with the same word. Here Nietzsche says that the human must make up stories before thinking is possible. People make up stories making two cases identical, even though they are not so in reality. Such stories are therefore something more fundamental than—and comes before—what we do when we consciously, for reasons of purpose, for example, look at two different cases as if they were the same.

Nietzsche therefore sees this as a shortcoming of language. But with the knowledge we now have about how consciousness' formation of thoughts is precisely based on "story-telling" in the languageless communication between mother and child, among other things to be able to create a self, it is not at all certain that it is a weakness. The formation of a consciousness is a seamless continuation of the emotional communication, via the "story-telling", and the narrative. The new neurobiological knowledge teaches us that we become thinking subjects by first being helped to make stories, or in other words: to create narratives in which we ourselves are included.

Skjervheim therefore warns against relying completely on pure, logical thinking when it leads to conclusions that contradict common sense. We can now supplement such a warning with the help of this new knowledge from the combination of neurobiology and psychoanalysis: Mental models that are supposed to explain

---

6 A thorough account of the transition from understanding in the form of stories to understanding in the form of abstract patterns can be found in Katherine Nelson's book *Language in Cognitive Development. Emergence of the Mediated Mind* (Nelson 1996)

something are often coherent and mutually consistent constructions. But they are formed as parts of processes that mostly escape our awareness. We cannot ignore the possibility that in these more or less conscious processes we manage what language cannot, namely distinguish between two different cases even if they are described with the same word. This is important knowledge to bring further, for example, when we are going to use diagnoses or other forms of categorization. I will come back to this below.

An example: Mentalization

In the previous chapter, I presented the recent neurobiological research on how the brain develops in the first years of life. This research has been continued by several others. A contribution that is particularly interesting in this context is that made by the Hungarian-British psychologist and psychoanalyst Peter Fonagy. He has discovered something he calls the *interpersonal interpretative mechanism* (IIM) (Fonagy 2006: 153). It assumes that through the interaction that takes place between mother and child, and eventually with others, we develop an ability to interpret other people's expressions based on what we assume they feel and think. At the same time, we learn to evaluate our own inner feelings so that we can convey them in factual language, both to others and to ourselves (for example by saying "Now I got sad"). This ability to link thinking to the emotional and other processes of which we are not aware, also in relationships between people, Fonagy calls *mentalization*. He and his colleagues have developed it into a method in psychotherapy that they call mentalization-based therapy.

But this is not only relevant for psychiatry. In fiction, theatre and film, this is precisely what is often going on: communication between people who tell both us and the fictional co-characters something about what happens beneath the surface of consciousness. A good writer is one who gives us as readers and audience an experience of recognition in our own minds.

Consciousness tries to understand

The shaping of conscious thoughts that we express in words is our attempt to create an order that we can convey to others, whether it is to a real other, or it is to an imagined other, as when we think alone. Consciousness tries to understand what it stands before[7], either to search for justifications, find answers to questions or find out what is the proper way to solve a task. Human consciousness has been developed through evolution, and it helps us to deal more purposefully and together with others. But as we have seen, consciousness is also created in the individual through an emotional communication, which in turn is linked to unconscious, neurobiological processes. On the one hand, then, consciousness tries to create explanations for what we call our thoughts; on the other hand, these efforts have been created in an organism where emotions and unknown processes take place all the time. In the previous chapter I described consciousness as the organism's communication department: It tries to present what happens internally in the organism as something understandable and free of contradictions, while what actually happens behind what is presented externally is both full of contradictions, emotional and partly chaotic.

Both consciousness and an organisation's communication department want what is conveyed in words to reach the recipient, and then the words must point to something that both parties have a shared experience of. And they must be put together in a way, with a language, with its logic and grammar, which allows one party to be as sure as possible that what he says, or writes (or thinks), is understood by the other as the sender wants it should be understood.

There is also a difference between forming thoughts on your own and having a conversation with someone else. When I form my own thoughts, there is no one else to correct me. Forming thoughts is a subjective activity. At the same time, it must be communicable; it must therefore be understandable in some sense of the word, it cannot

---

7 The German (and Scandinavian) word for understand is "verstehen", that is, to stand before.

be completely incoherent. Art experiments with precisely this. The artist sends out some words, images or other expressions where the context can be ambiguous, so that something new can arise for the recipient. In professional help, however, there is sometimes little room for such ambiguity. Here, it may rather be very important that what is communicated is unambiguous and is received exactly as intended, such as in acute situations or major interventions in the body or mind. At other times, it may be both possible and desirable—and perhaps necessary—to meet those who are to be helped, and people, with other sides of the human than just with an unambiguous language, it may be humour, a poem, music or others ways in which the emotions are also involved. This is something that an experienced professional helper uses in situations where professional language is not sufficient, for example because strong emotions stand in the way.

All formation of thoughts is thus necessary subjective, since it takes place inside our heads. At the same time, thoughts have no meaning if we cannot formulate them in words, even just for ourselves, which must be understood and recognized. The thought models that are communicated must therefore fulfil some common rules about consistency. We need to be able to share our thoughts with each other. Skjervheim (and others) called this an *intersubjectivity*. There must be "a subject with whom I share this world" (Skjervheim 1959: 44). In our own thoughts we are lonely, but through language and in a shared world of practice we can participate with our own thoughts, so that they give meaning to others and thus also to ourselves. It is precisely this experience that is easily forgotten when professional practice is subjected to a goal management or reporting practice that is designed outside of this daily community of practice. I'll come back to that soon.

Clearly, we constantly need to be reminded that thoughts are subjective, that they arise and exist in the individual's head. We can see many examples of a form of "objectification" of thoughts, i.e. a belief in, or a conscious exploitation of, that as soon as some thoughts are expressed, they have a status and a validity as if they were something objectively granted. Such an objectification of (the subjective) thoughts is perhaps even more dangerous today than it was in Skjervheim's time. We can see that in both religion and politics. When we express our thoughts to others, we often find it easy to adopt a "scientific", "objective" language. As, for instance, when a politician or a manager in a company calls an exploitation or a deterioration of nature 'development', 'value creation' or 'innovation'. Such use of words can trigger others, and perhaps be experienced as an offense because an expression of a subjective thought is perceived as objectively true when it is expressed, and even more so if it is put on paper. Such experiences show how much power lies in a subjective statement. Other examples can be reviews of literature or other art, which can have major financial consequences for those who are reviewed. What is easily forgotten, by all parties, is that every verbal statement is created in a context, not just a textual and social context, but also an emotional, biological and physical context. This context is really the entire reality in which the language is created. Outside the context, the statement easily takes on a different meaning. Let's take a closer look at this.

Categories and diagnoses

"I think, therefore I am," said the 17th-century philosopher René Descartes. He laid the foundations for a systematic thinking that was a success for the discoveries of the Enlightenment and for the whole of modern science. The Enlightenment was the detachment of thinking from the old authorities, both ecclesiastical and secular, and their monopoly on what was truth. Humans discovered that they could understand the world around them on their own, by observing and using their own abilities for logical thinking. It was the beginning of what we know today as science and the scientific method. Here Descartes was one of the great founders (Eriksen 1994: 308–321).

The disadvantage of this method, which Descartes laid the

foundation for, was that only what could be rationally described in words was let through the eye of the needle. One area where we currently see this disadvantage is the use of diagnoses and other categorizations of individual cases in professional help. Diagnoses are useful, important and in many cases necessary in order to manage, finance and roughly sort the services to be provided, for the benefit of the person being helped. But at the same time, there is a danger that all cases with the same diagnosis are treated the same, even if they are different cases and should have been treated differently.

Here we are again back to what Skjervheim writes about in his essay "Invitation to (cultural(?)) suicide?", and to which I referred above: If we are not aware that we must constantly use the same word in different cases and instead use language as if it were reality, we cannot, in the utmost logical consequence, really trust anything that is described in words, whether written or spoken. The whole thing then becomes a question of power, where whoever has the power of definition also decides how we should understand the world.

Skjervheim's answer to how this can be avoided is to start from the fact that we are independent thinking subjects, who also use our judgment when we have to orientate ourselves in the world. If we now ask what is really meant by "judgement" here, as we saw above, we get the help from neurobiology, which can tell us that the conscious formation of thoughts we mobilize when we have to understand a situation or another person, starts with underlying processes that are not conscious. Neurobiology thus points beyond its own reach: Since it is consciousness that is the tool, it cannot explain everything that happens behind this same consciousness. Therefore, different ways of thinking and using words than the natural sciences do, can help us to get a common understanding of what is happening. It can be the language and approaches of the humanities,[8] but it can also be non-scientific language, not least in the form of stories.

---

8 Phenomenology and hermeneutics are examples of such languages and approaches in the human sciences.

A wise practitioner with practical experience, and who has thus developed what is called a professional judgement, knows that each individual case is unique, and that diagnoses and other forms of categorization must not be given too much weight; indeed, that in some cases they can even stand in the way of good treatment. Precisely in such cases, it is only the specific individual case and the direct meeting with the person in need of help, both before and after a diagnosis is made, that can give the professional practitioner the necessary knowledge to find the best possible way forward. A concrete individual case can never be fully expressed by words alone, precisely because language is so much more limited than reality. A diagnosis, or any other form of categorization or generalization (for example "refugees" or "Muslims"), has a very limited meaning on its own. The words only gain meaning when they are put in a context. And most of this context cannot initially be described in words; it can only be experienced in a physical reality. This does not prevent us from having to constantly try to put such experiences into words in order to communicate with others. That is why a good, professional helper must also be able to communicate emotionally and with more than rational professional language. It is necessary to be able to relate to individual cases as unique, as something different from other individual cases even if they are initially described with the same words.

The power of storytelling: Svetlana Alexievich

The Belarusian journalist and author Svetlana Alexievich received the Nobel Prize in Literature in 2015. One of the books for which she has become famous is entitled *The Unwomanly Face of War* (Alexievich 2017). Here she writes about conversations with many women who actively participated in the Second World War for the Soviet Union. The Second World War was the greatest national trauma for the people who were then part of the Soviet Union, as the First World War was for Germany and France. The war cost the Soviet Union approximately 20 million human lives. In the introduction to the book, Svetlana Alexievich tells how, in her meetings with these women, she was struck by both how different women's narratives from the war were from men's, and how unfamiliar these narratives were. She writes in the introduction:

> "Women's stories are different and about different things. "Women's war" has its own colors, its own smells, its own lighting, and its own range of feelings. Its own words. There are no heroes and incredible feats, there are simply people who are busy doing inhumanly human things. And it is not only they (people!) who suffer, but the earth, the birds, the trees. All that lives with on earth with us. They suffer without words, which is still more frightening.
>
> But why? I asked myself more than once. Why, having stood up for and held their own place in a once absolutely male world, have women stood up for their history? Their words and feelings? They did not believe themselves. A whole world is hidden from us. Their war remains unknown...
>
> I want to write the history of that war. A women's history." (Alexievich 2017: xvi).

Earlier in this chapter we highlighted the narrative as the first way of using words. The new knowledge about brain development shows that it is precisely stories that create a self, as something persistent from one moment to the next (Schore 1994: 494). Alexievich reproduces the women's stories about the war. She emphasizes that it is the same war as the one that men have told about at all times, and which have become the official versions—with victories and heroes— but these too are stories, and thus no more real. At the same time, it is the stories that shape society. Today's society is told in different ways, and politics often becomes a competition for which narrative gets the most support. In professional practice, stories can also have great power. Established narratives about the sick, those in need of help and children can easily become a guide for understanding them.

Then it is important to be reminded that even if we cannot detach ourselves from the stories, there are always more stories about the same child or the same adult. And not one of them is entirely true.

Myths and religion are part of a cultural heritage with stories about people and their lives. Science also meets us as stories. It is inevitable. Because as Nietzsche also had to acknowledge: before something is thought, it must have been made up (see page 29).

But what happens when the myths take over, when they replace the reality we are all a part of, before we compose, and before we think? We have seen that our ability to use our consciousness to understand the world around us develops in an emotional communication and the regulation of emotions that we learned in the very first years of life, first with the help of our mothers, then from others and gradually increasing by own help, but still never completely without help from others. It is therefore not entirely irrelevant to ask: Did a fanatical religious or a political extremist get the help with affect regulation that belongs to the first two years of life? However, such questions will primarily be retrospective; a lack of care in childhood can undoubtedly be one of several factors that make a person develop into being violent. It will be more important to ask the question more generally, and directed forward in time: When more children grow up with a lack of care, won't that lead to a society with more uncontrolled emotions, and thus more violence?

Emotions are therefore important mediators of what lies deeper than and outside consciousness, but which is called forth by either external impressions or forgotten memories. But at the same time, we must remember that "emotions" is just a word, that is, a result of an attempt to be described by "someone else", in this case the consciousness, with the limitations inherent in this effort. If we rather think of emotions as internal, neurobiological processes that we can feel because they "tickle" our consciousness somewhere in there, it might be easier to imagine how what we call emotions can be important carriers of knowledge that have not yet reached the surface of consciousness, but may be on their way there.

Chapter 3:
From experience
to description

Husserl's worry

Chapter 1 describes the new knowledge about brain development. We saw how important the early interaction with a caregiver is, in a context of goodness, for the brain to be able to reach the potential that evolution has given it. We further saw how consciousness arises as a continuation of an emotional communication, and how we eventually get an experience of our own self, as a narrative in which we can see the difference between the I and the others. Chapter 2 follows this up by describing how consciousness can shape thoughts with the help of words in a way that enables us to communicate with each other in an understandable way, despite the fact that we are basically separated from each other, both as individual bodies and in each our worlds of thought.

In these discussions, the difference—and the relationship—between the objective and the subjective has been a central theme. The human body is obviously something that is objectively given, independent of the subject. The subject is precisely established in an already objectively existing body. But the subject also gets its own understanding of itself and its body, which is something different from the understanding that an outsider, for example a professional helper, gets. Such professional understandings are also subjective. At best, they are intersubjective, that is, we experience that we can share our subjective thoughts with others, often as a result of being in the same part of reality. Behind it all lies a material, objective reality, prior to any theorizing and understanding. What access do we have to this objective reality, in science and in everyday life?

This is a core question which in itself has led to a lot of thinking throughout the ages, both in our own and in other cultures. Here I would like to highlight a thinker who is particularly important in this context. It is the philosopher Edmund Husserl (1859–1938). Interestingly, like Freud, he was born into a Jewish family in the dual monarchy of Austria-Hungary in what is now the Czech Republic, just three years later than Freud, in the town of Proßnitz, now called Prostějov, just 90 kilometres away from where Freud was born. But while Freud, as a doctor, chose an objective perspective as a starting point in his research (but eventually realized the necessity of the subjective perspective by emphasizing the patients' own narratives), Husserl (after studying mathematics) chose a subjective starting point. He saw this as the only thing possible and it became the basis for his own contribution to philosophy, which is called phenomenology, and which will be presented in more detail later in this chapter. But Husserl also saw the significance of the objectively given reality that exists independently of the subject. In the last years of his life, he was concerned about the state of the sciences in Europe, also about how his own phenomenology was continued. He expresses this in the book *The Crisis of European Sciences and Transcendental Phenomenology* (Husserl 1970).

Husserl describes how the sciences, as he saw them at the time, had become self-absorbed and had lost the unifying function of creating meaning for people, a function they had had from antiquity up to and including the Enlightenment. He believed that the sciences had lost touch with the reality that they explored, and in which people lived, and instead were only concerned with their own theories and the excellence of human rationality. He believed that in recent years the sciences had developed into an intellectual game—at best a set of fragmented explanations for the observations of the individual sciences—without contact with the experiences of ordinary people. In a lecture in Vienna in 1935, which became a prelude to the book, he says:

"Is not the case that what we have presented here [the self-understanding of the sciences] is something rather inappropriate for our time, an attempt to rescue the honour of rationalism, of "enlightenment", of an intellectualism which loses itself in theories alienated from the world, with its necessary evil consequences such of a superficial lust for erudition and an intellectualistic snobbism? Does this not mean that we are being led again into the fateful error of believing that science makes man wise, that it is destined to create a genuine and contented humanity that is master of its fate? Who would still take such notions seriously today?" (Husserl 1970: 289–290)

In other words, the scientists have lost contact with the world around them and see themselves as the clergy of rationalism, as the saviours of the world, an opinion they are otherwise quite alone in.

Reality, on the other hand, is something that exists before all theories, it is a "pre-theoretical" reality, which is something other than what the sciences describe in their theories. This actual reality Husserl called the *lifeworld*. It is in the world of life that we as humans live and make our experiences, which we then take with us into the world of concepts and systems that we construct with our thinking, both in the sciences and in everyday life:

"...the everyday surrounding world of life is presupposed as existing – the surrounding world in which all of us (even I who am now philosophizing) consciously have our existence; here are also sciences, as cultural facts in this world, with their scientists and theories. In this world we are objects among objects in the sense of the life-world, namely, as being here and there, in the plain certainty of experience, before anything that is established scientifically, whether in physiology, psychology, or sociology. On the other hand, we are subjects for this world, namely, as ego-subjects experiencing it, contemplating it, valuing it, related to it purposefully...." (Husserl 1970, 104–105)

Husserl believed that the sciences had forgotten the pre-theoretical world of life which is also their source of knowledge, and that the scientists only moved in their own, closed and subjective rational thoughts.

Science's image of reality is not a one-to-one mapping. Among other things, we have seen that science, which is the result of thinking, is subjective (at best intersubjective) and rational, while reality is the opposite: objective and non-rational, because it is not thought by anyone. This realization was precisely what led Husserl to what he called phenomenology: The only thing we can know as subjects in this world is how this world appears to us, as various phenomena. Language and knowledge must therefore always rest on an assumption—which must always remain an assumption—that we generally have a common understanding of the reality in which we live and work, and which we describe and refer to among each other.

But, as Husserl himself points out, this does not mean that the real, objectively given world does not exist. On the contrary: we live in it, but we can only understand it from each of our subjective perspectives, and from these subjective understandings the individual sciences are built. What Husserl reminds us of in the quotes above is that the sciences are themselves activities in the lifeworld and are thus encompassed by it. As we touched on in chapter 2, an understandable description of reality can only make sense between people who are in a more or less common lifeworld, with some common experiences. Science, where we as I-subjects "experience the world, think about it, evaluate it and relate to it with our purposes", as Husserl says, thus becomes both important, useful and necessary, but at the same time something that always takes place, and which takes place in an objectively existing lifeworld, where we are, as Husserl says in the quote above, "objects among other objects [...] with a pure and immediate experience", before any theories are made.

In his essay *Spring*, the novelist Karl Ove Knausgård reflects on these two worlds like this:

> "More and more often it occurs to me that we live in two realities, one that is physical, material, biological, chemical, the world of objects and bodies, which perhaps we may call reality of the first order, and one that is abstract, immaterial, linguistic and cognitive, the world of relationships and social interactions, which we might call reality of the second order. The first reality is governed by absolute laws which leave no doubt – water freezes at a certain temperature, the apple detaches from the tree when it reaches a certain weight and the gust of wind attains a certain strength, it falls to the ground at a certain velocity, and the impact with the ground causes the flesh of the fruit beneath the skin to bruise in a certain pattern – while the other reality is relative and negotiable. This would have been easy to grasp if the two worlds existed side by side, but of course that's not how things are. One world exists within the other..." (Knausgård 2018: 61).

Now let us take a closer look at this difference between these two worlds.

Putting reality into words

The abstract, logical language in, for example, any report from or description of, reality, is only like single points in a continuous, material reality. Using only rational language in communication with each other can be compared to two prisoners communicating with each other by means of primitive knocking signals, but the difference is that—unlike the prisoners, albeit perhaps with some effort—we can go out into the material reality that also the other part inhibits. This will make it possible to communicate over a much wider spectrum than we can through such single signs, which also a rational language consists of.

A description of a reality can never replace a direct experience of the same reality. Reading a map can never replace walking in the terrain, no matter how detailed the map is made (and no matter how much pleasure we can get from reading a map). This is what Husserl criticized the scientists for: They had lost contact with the lifeworld, the everyday reality, where we humans make the experiences that are later formulated as scientific theories.

Let us add to this the more recent knowledge from neurobiology presented earlier in this book. "Consciousness is the surface of the psychic apparatus," said Freud (2014: 488). The knowledge that has come to us later has taught us that consciousness is shaped in interaction with others, while at the same time it is connected to underlying neurobiological processes. We have also learned that we humans have an ability to communicate over a wider spectre than through spoken and written words, especially when we are physically in the same place. When Freud talks about "the unconscious", it can mislead us to think of something potentially conscious, something of the same "stuff" as thoughts. This is how he also saw it himself (Freud 1957). With what we know today, it would be more correct not to call it the unconscious, but to see it as neurobiological processes that do not reach consciousness. The pure and immediate experience that Husserl talks about, the one that we have when we are objects among other objects in the lifeworld, consists in being part of a biological and physical reality. The thoughts and assessments that the I-subject makes as a result of such a pure and immediate experience, however, are something else, as I specified at the beginning of the previous chapter (and which Knausgård describes even better in the quote above). It is what is expressed by means of conscious thoughts that have been put into words.

The German mathematician Georg Cantor (1845–1918) has described both the qualitative and the quantitative difference between reality and any description of it. Reality constitutes what we call a continuum. This means that it is "seamlessly" connected, in both time and space. However, any description of reality, which may consist of words, numbers and other symbols, does not constitute a continuum. Rather, they are single points, which can be numbered – preferably in an infinitely long list (for example, the entire sequence of numbers 1, 2, 3, etc. *ad infinitum*). Every description we may make of reality can be ordered similarly by such a numbered list.

What Georg Cantor did was to introduce a measure of the size of quantities, even those that are infinitely large. He called these measurements *cardinal numbers*. Cardinal numbers do not always behave like ordinary numbers, as for example in the expression below.[9] This expression says something about the relationship between the cardinal number of a continuum, c, such as material reality, and the cardinal number of the set of all words, concepts and symbols that is made and put together, in other words everything that can be numbered, and which we call n. As mentioned, this is also an infinitely large quantity, since the series of numbers never ends, but Cantor found that the cardinal number c must still be greater than the cardinal number n, and not only that, but also that

$$c - n = c$$

Put into words, this formula says that if we extract countable elements from a continuum—as many as we want, and preferably using a method that extracts an infinite number (for example using an algorithm in a computer program)—then we are anyway still left with a continuum.

So what does this mean in our everyday life? Let's go back to the professional helper. If we start from the helper's experiences with those who are helped, in their shared reality, and from these experiences select certain words that can be written and numbered, for example in a detailed report, the experiences the helpers are left with, but which are not included in any evaluation forms, is still an "as big" infinite reality as it was before these forms were created

---

9 If the two symbols in the expression had represented ordinary numbers, the arithmetic rules say that the symbol n must be zero, which in this case it is not.

(namely a continuum). This is because the helpers and the helped belong to the same biological and relational continuous reality, while the report forms belong to a subjectively constructed and numbered description of reality.

What gives the helpers an advantage over their leaders or politicians is that they are physically in the same reality as the helped. They are thus able to understand them with a greater part of the human potential to understand something than those who are not present and who are limited to the part of these processes that are communicated verbally. As we have seen earlier in this book, this potential is great; it is partially unconscious, but it is equally capable of communicating with the conscious part of our minds.

To summarize: Cantor's theory of cardinal numbers can be used to describe the difference between the real (continuous) world, where we ourselves are "objects among other objects", on the one hand, and all thoughts that some subject puts words (that can be numbered) and texts on, on the other. The symbol c in the equation above denotes the size of the real world, what Husserl called the lifeworld: the physical, biological and relational reality of which we are all part and make our experiences. The symbol n, in turn, becomes a symbol for the size of the set of all words in the world and all the ways of putting these together – all that has been, all that is, and all that will come: words in stories, in documents, in science, in everyday conversation and in all digital information, including the computer program in a robot. The equation above says that if in the real world we identify individual experiences and individual cases, as in an evaluation form, a legal text, a computer program (or in a religious scripture, for that matter), what remains in this reality—i.e. that which is *not* identified and described—is just as much and as large as it was before this was done.

Transcendental materialism

Husserl called his last book *The Crisis of European Sciences and Transcendental Phenomenology*. When he called his phenomenology transcendental (which means something that transcends our experiences), it was because he saw no other possibility than that the ego-subject and its consciousness must be established first, in order to be able to study objective reality, including itself as a subject. The fundamental prerequisite for understanding the world, Husserl believed, is not the world that is objectively there, but that there is a conscious ego-subject who can experience it. Without such a subject, no science, although the world is there ever so much. The conscious ego-subject must therefore first be assumed to exist, an assumption that transcends our experiences of the world. That is why he called his phenomenology transcendental (Husserl 1970: 98).

This book has a different starting point. The knowledge that has come forth during the last 30–35 years gives us the opportunity to reverse the order of the subject and the material world in which it is located: The ego-subject is not presupposed to exist, instead it emerges gradually within the lifeworld. In a scientific consideration (and therefore not, for example, a religious) we only know the material world—including the biological world we are born into as individuals—as objectively existing. Chapter 1 describes how a subject is gradually formed within the individual body, as a self and an I, through an emotional interaction, primarily with the mother, during the first two years of life. Part of this self is our consciousness, but to the self, or I, we also count some of the processes that do not reach consciousness, but which nevertheless contribute to making us who we are, both in others' and in our own eyes. Consciousness is only a limited part of the neurobiological processes, and there is therefore much in these processes that we will never be able to become aware of. When these non-conscious processes present themselves from time to time and appear in our consciousness, the rational thinking is only of limited help. But we can still recognize them in other forms of expression: as something the body remembers, as art that gives us a kind of recognition, or as an echo in inherited myths, including religion, which have both long historical roots in our culture and mental roots in our mind. We have therefore learned to put words to such experiences by transcending the rational and linguistically expressed cognition. Here, neurobiology also points beyond its own reach, precisely because as a science it is limited to using consciousness as a tool. I would therefore call such a view of the world a *transcendental materialism*. This may seem somewhat unclear and difficult for now, but I will try to make it clearer in the following.

The word "transcendental" is important here. A "pure" materialism would easily be associated with a pure objectivism, that is, a purely rationalist view of reality, which limits itself to the knowledge that the conscious formation of thoughts can understand. Then we can easily end up in the "American doctrine of behaviourism" that Freud warned against (page 11). But we are also subjects, who have an alternating contact with that in us that is not conscious. Therefore, while the word "materialism" refers to the fact that we do not know anything that objectively exists outside the material world, we are nevertheless as subjects on a constant search for that which cannot be recognized consciously, and which we become familiar with from time to time in various ways. It is our fate that our ability to understand material reality is limited by our consciousness. As a result of this, we constantly go beyond rational language in our attempts to orient ourselves in reality, by using other sources of insight than precisely the cognitions of consciousness. In other words: Since our consciousness is a limited part of the reality we find ourselves in, it will constantly try to transcend what it can understand, but which it can recognize in one way or another.

Science and religion

Towards the end of the 20th century, many believed that science would render all religion redundant. Such an assumption was part of what we can call "the hubris of rationality", which in many ways characterized the entire 20th century, and which, among others, also characterized Husserl and Freud. Today we see that religion is by no means being replaced by science, neither in other cultures nor in our own. It can only mean that science and the knowledge it provides do not fully cover people's need to create order and meaning in their thoughts and emotions. As long as we recognize that there is much more than what rational thinking can put into words, rationality will also have its limitations in giving people the answers they seek. It is also connected to the fact that we as humans seek more than which meets specific purposes. We also search for a meaning, or a connection, in existence, and here people have always made non-scientific constructions, not only with words—such as in inherited, mythical stories—but also in the form of art and experiences in nature and other expressions and activities that connect consciousness to what lies "under" it, such as meditation, yoga, mindfulness, etc.

Science is limited to the range of rational thought. The more recent knowledge that thinking is a neurobiological activity that is continuously linked to far more extensive activities in the body places rational thinking in a larger context. The development of new knowledge in this area is a kind of parallel to the development in astronomy: From believing that humans were the centre of the universe, we now know that we live on a planet that is one among several planets in our solar system, which in turn is one among several solar systems in a larger star system, and which again is only one among billions of star systems. If we go into our body, we now know that consciousness can be localized to a limited part of our neuro-system, and that most of the body's functions manage perfectly well without the help of this. If we then go from this biological observer perspective to the perspective of the conscious subject, it is no wonder that from time to time we can sense that consciousness works in surroundings that we, precisely because they lie outside of consciousness, will never be able to understand.

Throughout human history, there is nothing that can compare with religions as the most universal and meaningful attempts to find words and expressions for just such sensations. The fact that we will never be able to come up with any verbal description that fully covers these sensations, neither with scientific nor with religious texts, is due to something as simple as that the combined scope of all verbal explanations (what can be numbered) can never reach the extent of the objectively given reality (which is a non-countable continuum).

A strong belief in the self-sufficiency of rationality is often connected with an equally strong belief in the self-sufficiency of words. However, some people lose the first belief without losing the second, allowing, for example, religious texts to replace scientific ones, instead of seeing both as always inadequate attempts to express human experience and imagination. This can, as we know, be a source of major conflicts and in some cases have violent expressions.

The monorational shelters

Earlier in this chapter we saw how Edmund Husserl expressed his worries about how the scientists were losing touch with the reality they explored, and in which people lived, and were instead only concerned with their own theories and with the excellence of human rationality.

Husserl criticized scientists for closing themselves into what we could call their own shelters where they could cultivate their rational theories and concepts for themselves, while they, with the privileges that traditionally had accompanied that of being a scientist, could leave it to others, who were outside these shelters to deal with the lifeworld as such. We may thus view such shelters that are constructed within the wider lifeworld, as being *monorational*.

Within a monorational shelter, the world is assumed to be understandable. It is probably related to an imagination—and an expectation—of having control. The world can be understood with the use of words, or more precisely a finite number of individual categories and concepts which, ideally, are put together into a logically consistent description of reality in the sense of being free of internal contradictions. Such descriptions are usually based on scientifically produced knowledge, but it can alternatively take the form of religious or other ideological (as well as conspiracy) thought constructions. From these consistent constructions of words and concepts, answers to the tasks and questions that arise at any time are derived. In principle, all tasks and challenges can be solved both within and with the help of the same monorational understanding of reality. Sense impressions and experiences that do not fit into the consistent model of reality are placed outside the shelter and thus considered irrational and rejected as irrelevant.

Outside these monorational shelters lies the world where we live our daily lives. Here we have all, from birth and through the first years of childhood, learned an immediate and more physical approach to the world. In this approach, the world is basically larger and more complex than any possible understandable model or description can cover. The individual subject connects to the world through relationships with other people and through the wide variety of communication forms, each with their own form of rationality. These relationships are fundamentally ethical, in the sense that every person is at the mercy of other people's kindness and hospitality, regardless of both their own and others' intellectual abilities and skills. The individual makes its way through everyday language that is situational, where what is said in one situation may well be incompatible with what is said in another. Communication initially occurs in physical proximity with others, but can also be continued in various forms at a distance.

Eventually (and we are still outside the monorational shelters), concrete and defined tasks appear that must be solved. A logically consistent understanding of the problem is then established and a rational solution to the present task is developed. In the next round, a new, limited task appears, which again gets its logical understanding model with the resulting solution. But each task and each situation has its own unique logic and rationality. This approach may thus be named *multirational*, as a contrast to the monorational shelter.

Research on the brain's early development (among others, Schore 1994) suggests that all people from birth and in early childhood have what I have here named a multirational approach to the world.

Then, eventually, and especially if one belongs to the privileged, one can seek refuge in a monorational shelter, where one is not too much disturbed by the realities of life, such as births and caring for others than oneself, often helped by existing social gender roles. This can make the monorational shelter a good place to be for those who have the opportunity.

Belonging to the privileged therefore makes it easier to hold on and cultivate a monorational approach. It also means that when privileges disappear, such an approach, out in the open lifeworld, can work less well. Perhaps it is some of this that we see in men who experience having lost the privileges that traditionally came with their gender?

We cannot of course, even after what has been written above, generalize and say that the monorational shelter is the refuge of men, while women are out in the life world and from there apply a multirational approach. Nevertheless, and as already indicated, we can say that there is a gender dimension in this landscape: On a macro level, we can say that traditionally men have had a greater opportunity than women to shield themselves from a diverse and partly incomprehensible lifeworld, in order to enter into a constructed and comprehensible monorational shelter and stay there, at least for a while.

Back to the lifeworld: Edith Stein

Edith Stein was born in 1891 in the city of Breslau, which was then located in Germany, but which today is called Wrocław and is located in Poland. She was born into a Jewish family as the youngest of seven children. Her father was a businessman, but when Edith was only three years old, he died suddenly of a stroke. The mother had to take over the business to feed the family at the same time as she fulfilled the role of mother. She gave her children a very loving but strict Jewish upbringing (Posselt 2005). Edith received top grades throughout her schooling. She began studying in Göttingen, eventually under Edmund Husserl. She was admitted as a doctoral student with Husserl as supervisor. When the First World War broke out, she interrupted her studies and volunteered for the Red Cross, where she cared for soldiers with epidemic diseases. In 1916, Husserl was offered a professorship in Freiburg, and he asked his favourite student, Edith Stein, to become his assistant, which she accepted. In Freiburg, she completed her doctoral thesis *On the Problem of Empathy*.

In her dissertation, she showed that she fully mastered Husserl's phenomenological method, which he had developed over a long period of time into a rather complex system of concepts, definitions and methodological techniques. In her thesis she saw the experienced, emotional empathy as a problem in Husserl's phenomenological conceptual apparatus, because it did not fit into any of the existing categories. She came to the conclusion that it had to form a category by itself (Stein 1989: 11). What created the biggest problem in the description of the emotional experience in a phenomenological framework of understanding was that there had to be a connection between a bodily and a mental sensation, which until then was new in Husserl's method.[10] Here she anticipated later phenomenological contributions, such as the French philosopher Maurice Merleau-Ponty's pointing out the importance of the body in people's lives and understanding of the world, and not least Husserl's own, but later, concept of the lifeworld.

In her dissertation, she showed an insight that had much in common with that of Sigmund Freud, but which she had clearly developed completely independently of him. She saw the importance that past experiences can have an impact on human experiences of the world, even if they are in a mental background to recent experiences. She termed these experiences "the mode of non-actuality", something Freud called the unconscious around the same

---

10 The source here is the English translation of the thesis (Stein 1989), where the translator, Waltraut Stein, who is also Edith Stein's grandniece, has also written an informative introduction for readers who, like the present author, are not one hundred percent familiar with Husserl's conceptual apparatus.

time. In that way, Edith Stein went beyond Husserl's conceptual apparatus in the direction of Freud's (Stein 1989: xxiii).

Being a woman, it seemed impossible for Edith Stein to get a permanent position in the philosophical academic environment. She herself expressed that she did not find the truths and the meaning she was constantly searching for in philosophy. She converted to Catholicism in 1922, left university and began teaching at a Catholic girls' school. She also taught in teacher training, while also being an active writer, including translating the philosopher and theologian from the 13th century, Thomas Aquinas. She also visited her former teacher Husserl and dedicated an article to him for his 70th birthday in 1929 entitled "Husserl's Phenomenology and the Philosophy of St. Thomas Aquinas" (Posselt 2005: 74).

In several of her letters from this time, she expressed satisfaction that she now lived much more "here and now", in an everyday reality, in contrast to her previous life at the university. In a letter to a friend from this time, she writes:

> "Immediately before, and for a good while after my conversion, I was of the opinion that to lead a religious life meant one had to give up all that was secular and to live totally immersed in the thoughts of the Divine. But gradually I realized that something else is asked of us in this world and that, even in the contemplative life, one may not sever the connection with the world. I even believe that the deeper one is drawn into God, the more one must "go out of oneself"; that is, one must go to the world in order to carry the divine life into it." (Posselt 2005: 73)

When the Nazis came to power, she was deprived of her teaching position, and she sought refuge in a Carmelite monastery, first in Cologne, later in Echt in the Netherlands. In 1942 she was arrested and deported to Auschwitz. She was killed in a gas chamber, probably the same day she arrived (Posselt 2005: xvii).

Chapter 4:
The origins of ethics

Kant's proposal

How is ethics embodied in us? Immanuel Kant (1724–1804) is considered one of the founders not only of modern science, but also of our understanding of ethics. After proceeding as he usually did to acquire knowledge, namely by observing—in this case other people, but certainly also himself—and then testing out various hypotheses, he came up with a proposal that ethics is embodied in us humans in the form of a tacit "moral law". This moral law comes into play in situations where we are challenged to assess the needs of others against our own. It springs from a built-in ability to identify with the other, who in a given situation appeals to our goodness. This built-in, but wordless, moral law presents itself as a duty, but as a duty we ourselves have the freedom to follow or not to follow (Eriksen 1994: 413–415). Kant called this moral law "the categorical imperative", because it applies everywhere, and because it registers itself in us as something we must do. He formulated it as follows: "Act so that the maxim for your action could always simultaneously apply as a principle for the general legislation." The maxim for an action means an imaginary rule that an action actually follows (Eriksen 1994: 415). In other of Kant's proposals for the formulation of the moral law, it becomes even clearer that there is embedded in us both an idea of a human dignity for everyone as a value in itself and at the same time an idea of justice, among other things that I have no right to have privileges that others cannot have.

Chapter 1 describes how consciousness is formed as a seamless continuation of the emotional interaction between mother and child. The research on which this knowledge is based can also tell us that in this interaction empathy, trust and concern for others are learned before the ability to speak, think and reason (Schore 1994: 350–352). This new knowledge supplements and underpins Kant's assumptions about an embodied moral law. When we begin to form our own thoughts, the foundation for ethics is already laid. Later, thoughts of doing something good for others constantly move in and out of consciousness. It may disappear from consciousness for a while, only to reappear. This was a discovery Freud made with his patients, and which led him to introduce a term that lies between the conscious self and the unconscious, namely something unconscious in the I, which he in some contexts called the preconscious (Freud 1957).

As we become independent, thinking individuals, we also learn that a blind trust in anyone and everyone can be punishing. Such experiences then become correctives to the fundamentally positive attitude that is already embedded in us, through the emotional communication with the mother and eventually with others, where positive emotions are reinforced and negative emotions are met with empathy and comfort.

Here it must be added that children who do not get to experience the natural and normal interaction with a mother or another primary caregiver who is "good enough", as the English paediatrician and psychoanalyst David Winnicott expresses and describes it (Winnicott 1990a: 54; 1990b: 145), nor can such a fundamental trust be embodied. In such cases, professional therapists can try to "repair" the psychological damage caused by a lack of care. Allan Schore quotes his colleagues David Winnicott and Frances Tustin:

> "This context of psychopathogenesis is, again, characterized by Winnicott (1990b): If maternal care is not good enough, then the infant does not really come into existence, since there is no

continuity in being; instead, the personality becomes built on the basis of reactions to environmental impingement [p. 54]. Tustin (1981) refers to this impingement as a "psychological catastrophe," which is responded to by "autistic withdrawal" or "encapsulation," an innate defensive measure against bodily hurt that involves a "shutting out of mind" what can not be handled at the moment." (Schore 2002: 458).

For Kant, it was important to emphasize that the moral law is not a natural law that we are subject to as individuals. It only presents itself as a thought in consciousness; then we have to choose with our own thinking whether we want to follow this thought or not. When our thinking, perhaps on the basis of past experience, says that there is no reason to follow the spontaneous or unconscious impulse, it may be right not to do so. But we also make all our experiences that the "gut feeling" may still have been right, when we see it all in retrospect.

The role of gut feeling in our assessments of what is right and wrong has gained more scientific interest in recent years. Later research on the digestive system shows that the intestines are the organ in the body second only to the brain that has the most diverse network of nervous systems (Enders 2014: 132–133). There is talk of a "gut brain" which, based on experience, among other things, coordinates the entire digestion, and which communicates in a very advanced way with the "head brain". One difference between the two "brains" is that the "gut brain" exclusively controls muscles outside of our consciousness, while the "head brain" controls both with and without the involvement of consciousness. We gradually know more and more about the complex interaction between the conscious and the unconscious part of the nervous system in their collaboration on the control of our muscles and movements (Enders 2015: 134–138).

In this book, we will not deal with the "gut brain" any more, but simply stating that the knowledge of how the conscious and all that is not conscious is continuously connected neurobiologically—not only in the brain, but in the whole body—is in constant development. We realize, among other things, that the unconscious part of our nervous system also has a memory, in which consciousness is not involved. In this sense, there is an interesting connection between this unconscious part of the nervous system and what Freud called *id*, which was presented in chapter 1. This was also illustrated by Siri Hustvedt's story in the same chapter.

Terje Vigen

Norway's great playwright and poet Henrik Ibsen was born in 1828 and died in 1906. Through his poems and plays, he highlighted in several ways the embedded ethics in humans, as he and his contemporaries had learned from Kant, among others, that it could make itself felt and often create dilemmas in the meeting with society and in interpersonal relationships.

In the epic poem *Terje Vigen*[11], Ibsen tells of a man who lived "on the outermost, bare island", and who, in the war year 1809, rowed to Denmark to get grain for his small family, which, apart from himself, consisted of his wife and a small daughter. It was a risky crossing, because the English navy blocked the sea between Denmark and Norway, and when Terje was almost back home, he was overtaken by an English vessel under the command of a young officer of 18 who was out on his first mission. The precious cargo of grain was lost, and Terje was sent to prison in England for five years, until the war ended in 1814. When he returned home, both his wife and children had died of poverty and hunger because no one had taken care of them. After the worst grief, Terje starts life anew, like a lion. He becomes an old man in this deed, but is still marked by his great grief, and he is constantly gnawed by the thought of revenge. The poem's dramatic highlight is when Terje suddenly one day gets the opportunity to take revenge on the same English officer, who has now become an upper-class lord, and who comes into distress at sea with his yacht together with his wife and little daughter. Terje

---

11 For an English translation of the poem (by Fydell Edmund Garrett and Axel Gerhard Dehly), see http://www.identityofthesoul.com/Media/TerjeVigen_EnglishV-VanessaRedgrave.pdf

moves out to help the yacht, but suddenly discovers in the tumult of the storm who he is about to save. He realizes that not helping the lord in that case will also affect a mother and a daughter. The latter turns out to be called Anna, which was also the name of Terje's dead daughter.

At this moment, Terje Vigen is not acting as many, including himself, would have expected—and many would certainly also have shown an understanding based on his previous experiences— with a vengeance. Instead, he saves the young English family, and thus, Ibsen wants to say with this poem, he also "saves" himself as a human being. By not taking revenge, Terje found himself back again. Or to put it another way, he rediscovered the deeper part of himself, from the time before the tragedy struck him.

When Henrik Ibsen wrote the poem *Terje Vigen* in 1861, he himself was the father of small child. His son Sigurd, who was Henrik and Suzannah Ibsen's first child (and who also became their only one), was then two years old. Although it can of course only be speculation, we can imagine that Ibsen as a new father had gained some new experiences about, and a new insight into, what closeness to a child does to one's own mind, also below the surface of consciousness.[12] And Ibsen, as we know, developed an ability to bring out what moves beneath the surface of consciousness, better than most others.

When the English lord wants to thank his rescuer after all the drama, Terje Vigen replies that it was probably not himself who saved them, but rather their little daughter:

> The English lord and the lady came,
> And with them came many more;
> They wrung his hand and they blessed his name,
> As they stood in his humble door.

---

12 Behind this perhaps also lay a nagging bad conscience on the part of Henrik Ibsen: As a young pharmacist's apprentice in Grimstad, he had had a child with the pharmacist's maid. Ibsen took on the financial obligations that came with it, but rejected closer contact with this son (Figueiredo 2006:46–47)

For rescue brave from the waves fierce dread
They thanked him; but Terje smiled,
And gently stroking the golden head,
"The one you should thank stands here," he said,
"You were saved by the little child."

The diversity of ethics

This book began with the underlying ethics of professional helpers, who can trace their practice right back to as long as there have been humans, i.e. long before any science and any formulated ethics came into being. We have seen how recent knowledge about the development of the brain can tell us that shaping one's own, conscious thoughts is a seamless continuation of precisely these basic characteristics of being human. In a certain sense, we can say that ethics comes before knowledge, in fact as a prerequisite for it. But saying this can also easily lead to misunderstandings. Words like "ethics" and the words with which one has tried to describe ethics, such as "empathy", "trust", "responsibility", "respect", "openness", etc., yes, even "love", belongs to a later stage in a development, because such wordings are precisely attempts to draw (the continuous) thinking activity out of its pre-theoretical and pre-linguistic context and into (the countable) thoughts.

Seen from the outside, what happens in the brain in this early development can be described as neurobiological processes. Seen "from the inside", from the subject's own perspective, we sporadically become acquainted with these early experiences as thoughts move in and out of consciousness. There is "something" beneath consciousness. Freud experimented with words such as "the unconscious" and "id". The philosopher Emmanuel Levinas used, as we shall soon see, the expression "a past prior to all memory and all recall" (see page 65). Ibsen describes this in his narrative way. It is really quite obvious that we will never be able to fully describe what comes before any attempt to put something into words. We are facing part of an infinitely diverse and continuously objectively given reality that we can only experience from each of our subjective perspectives. And, as we have also touched on several times before, there are too few words for all the different experiences of this reality, so that the same word must always be used for different experiences. This is precisely why good professional practitioners can use the part of their human potential that lies below and before language and rational thinking, such as professional helpers who is with the helped on a daily basis, in contrast to their leaders, who are not. And that is precisely why it is important to have a knowledge of this human potential, not only for the professional practitioners, but perhaps even more so for those who have to make decisions higher up in the hierarchy.

This tells us that we should be cautious and reserved towards presentations of the subject area of ethics, if it is presented as a closed and consistent system of thinking and action, for example following the model from laws and regulations. As a field of knowledge, the same applies to ethics as to the professional care subjects and the knowledge they rely on: They have roots that go back to a pre-theoretical stage, both in evolution and in the individual's personal development. When helping other people becomes professionalised, it is absolutely necessary to put the knowledge into words. These constant efforts to bring to consciousness something that is embodied in more underlying processes, both in practice and in theory development, are absolutely necessary in such a professionalisation. Here, an academic knowledge must not be set up as a contradiction to a practically based knowledge. That is why it is so important that both professional knowledge and ethical knowledge retain the connection with their roots in material reality. To base one's actions only on the knowledge that can be expressed in words would mean cutting off these roots. The danger of what can be lost through a so-called academisation of ethics is therefore just as great as it is for all other practically oriented specialist knowledge.

The pre-theoretical ethics as I have tried to describe it in this book, with the support of neurobiology which complements the knowledge of philosophers such as Kant (see above) and

Levinas (see below), is thus something real, there are processes that can be registered in our nervous system. Any attempt to put it into words—for example, when Freud introduces the *id* (and the "superego"), or when we use words such as empathy, or mentalization, which were mentioned in the previous chapter—will always be a reduction of that which it attempts to describe, from something real existing to something constructed linguistically. Not only is there a reduction because our sense impressions and our languages are limited, there is also a reduction in that something universally human—that which begins with the emotional communication between mother and child as part of an objective reality—is described in a social and cultural context that can only be understood subjectively or at best intersubjectively.

In parts of the professional literature on ethics, a notion of one overarching, common human ethic is built up, which is often based on a respect for the inviolable intrinsic value of the individual human being. Declarations on human rights are also examples of this, as are the many basic professional ethical documents that have been created. In the specialist literature, reference is often made to Kant regarding our built-in idea of human intrinsic value and justice between people, in the form of a categorical imperative, as presented in the opening of this chapter. It is easy to understand the need for such a linguistic and comprehensible, and preferably scientific, presentation of what we call ethics. But both philosophers from earlier times and more recent neurobiological knowledge can tell us that behind all these attempts lies a common human, languageless source that is embodied in us, where consciousness does not sit in the driver's seat, but rather comes afterwards and tries to put the experiences into words. Rational, subjective and intersubjective explanations of the world we see around us can lead astray if detached from their original source. It also applies to attempts to create consistent systems of what we call ethics, whether they are now attempted to be described within a philosophical, a religious or a professional language. Such attempts can easily lead to equipping each world of thought with its own "ethics" ("intentional ethics", "consequential ethics", "Christian ethics", "Muslim ethics", etc., etc.). The starting point—the common humanity, the capacity for empathy and compassion—can thus easily get lost along the way.

Religion and ethics

As we have seen in the previous chapters, our thoughts come from sources "deeper down" in our minds, even in what is usually inaccessible to consciousness. Examples of such sources are inherited mythology in general and religion in particular. The Protestant theologian Knud E. Løgstrup (1905–1981) used the New Testament, not least the Sermon on the Mount (Matthew 5-7), as inspiration for his ethical texts. Løgstrup calls the positive, already embedded attitudes towards another human being the sovereign expression of life, expressed by trust, mercy and "open speech".

> "The expression of life cannot be applied. Principles, precepts, maxims can be applied. The sovereign expression of life cannot do that, it can only be fulfilled by me realizing myself in it. And it comes from the fact that it is souvereign. It does not fix the situation, but sets it in motion, transforms it, which is why the person must constantly play himself into it. (Løgstrup 2013: 97; translated from Danish by the present author).

Løgstrup is obviously trying to put into words something we know inside us, which is behind us, behind the I, and he sees this as "life itself", in which we are placed, and which makes us human. Immersing oneself into a conversation and let it go are situations we can all recognize ourselves in. For Løgstrup, such a situation is characterized by trust, mercy and "open speech", that is, "saying it like it is". A characteristic of the sovereign expression of life is that it is spontaneous. Being sceptical, not showing mercy or saying anything other than "as it is" is not spontaneous, it requires that we first think about it, or that there may be some obstacles in us that have an explanation in the past.

Another important source of inspiration for the ethics that are in dialogue with religion is the French philosopher Emmanuel Levinas (1906–1995). For Levinas, ethics is awakened in the encounter with "the face of the Other".[13,14]

Levinas is often cited as a central thinker in the ethics of the care professions. There are many in these professions who can recognize themselves in his descriptions of the experience of responsibility in the encounter with the Other. Levinas is precisely trying to put into words the pre-theoretical ethics. In the face of the Other lies an appeal for mercy. At the same time, Levinas goes a step further than simply describing the individual encounter with one other. He also describes how the encounter with "another Other", which he calls "the third", forces us to use language so that we, as subjects, can account for our choices and priorities by justifying them based on the idea of justice.

Levinas was also a recognized interpreter of scriptures in the Jewish religious community, and throughout his writing it becomes increasingly clear that "the Other" points towards a kind of god, but less bound to any specific religion.

The Belgian Catholic theologian Roger Burggraeve (b. 1942) collaborated with Levinas for several years and is among those who have passed on his thoughts. In an article (Burggraeve 2008) he points out that what Levinas calls "the Other" is also represented inside our own minds: In order for us to be able to be touched by the fate and suffering of the Other, we must be able to be "touchable" (Burggraeve 2008: 16). We must have internalized something that makes the encounter with the Other's face something more than just a registration of something that could just as well have been something other than a face. The meeting must hit something deeper down in us. Levinas writes several times that it hits a past that cannot be remembered. One place he describes

13 Note here the significance of the face, as was also mentioned in the emotional and unconscious communication between mother and infant, and which remains in the mind "a past prior to all memory and all recall" (see below).
14 For a further presentation of Levinas, see Aasland (2009).

metaphorically how meeting the Other is like first losing yourself and then finding yourself again, like this:

> "The evocation of maternity in this metaphor suggests to us the proper sense of oneself. The oneself cannot form itself; it is already formed with absolute passivity. ... This passivity is that of an attachment that has already been made, as something irreversibly past, prior to all memory and all recall. It was created in an irrecuperable time which the present, represented in recall, does not equal, in a time of birth or creation, of which nature or creation retains a trace, unconvertible into a memory. Recurrence is more past than any rememberable past, any past convertible into a present." (Levinas 1991: 104-105).

Freud talks about the *id* in the unconscious, an entity that calls itself forth and asserts itself in given situations. In his book *The Ego and the Id*, which was referred to in chapter 1, he mentions "a quantitative and qualitative 'something' in the course of mental events" (Freud 1961: 22). This detail may contain driving forces that the self does not notice. Only when the unconscious repression that the I exerts towards *the id* is made conscious, will this 'something' also become conscious.

The new knowledge about the development of the brain can make an important contribution to ethics, which at the same time establishes a connection between Freud and Levinas. In the care professions, there is a recognition in the close encounter with the person in need of help, and in the motivation to help that is awakened in such an encounter. Here we can imagine that what happens below consciousness is that the memory of the emotional interaction in the first years of life is recalled, the interaction that precisely laid the foundation for learning to empathize, a learning that in turn laid the foundation for the shaping of the self, thinking and later learning of what we call knowledge, including specialist knowledge. For, as described in the previous chapter, thinking and the formation of self-awareness can be understood as an exercise in conversing with an imagined other. The ethical appeal in the encounter with another is as if the other calls forth "the other in myself", which lies there, and which presents itself as an inner voice from "someone other than myself", as an echo of other persons, or perhaps rather the very first beginning of our own self, when the I came into being, in the emotional, unconscious interaction with the mother, in the meeting between two faces. We experience a form of recognition with something we were initially unaware of. Our body remembers something in a past that cannot be remembered by our conscious self. It has given us a human potential behind language and conscious knowledge, in the form of immediate impulses to comfort when someone is upset, to see others and provide reassurance when someone shows a need for it. At the same time, both research and experience show how things can go wrong when the attachment to a carer is not sufficient at the very first time.

Faced with what consciousness can only notice as sensations and recognitions in a past prior to all memory and all recall, a religious language can be of help to many, among other things to be able to put into words something that rational thinking cannot explain. Attempts to put into words a non-religious humanism in a similar way we also see examples of, as in all our attempts to put into words what a humanistic view of humanity is. The challenge for such attempts to put into words a general humanism is often to be able to go beyond a limited rationalism. In the same way as religions, a humanistic ethic will also be able to transcend rational language and use, for example, art, literature and inherited narratives as supplementary sources.

But whether such attempts to describe sensations from what lies beneath consciousness are clothed in a religious or a general humanistic language, the language will always have its limitations, as this was illustrated in the previous chapter as a qualitative difference between a continuous reality and all possible, but still countable, linguistic expressions: No matter how much of the objectively given reality we manage to put into words, there will always be an "equally large" part of reality left that we have not put into words, and which can only be experienced directly, in time and space, with precisely sensations, memories and physical presence.

Meeting people in need of help

Today's world faces new moral challenges. Thousands of people who are victims of war, chaos and misrule are seeking a better organized Europe. In the discussion about how this should be handled, the "idealists" are often pitted against the "realists". In the terminology of ethics, the "idealists" appeal to intentional ethics, by pointing to our immediate responsibility for people in need, which is expressed in a desire to help, while the "realists", to the extent that they refer to any ethics, support the ethics of consequences by point to the impossibility of helping "everyone". Another way to look at this is that we first meet these people in need of help emotionally, with the help of our embedded and embodied ability to empathize. It is therefore not in accordance with the roots of our own thinking to first meet them with a rational distance, for example to take as a starting point that migrants come to us as a result of a conscious plan to seek the best possible life. It would be more in keeping with the roots of our own thinking to begin with an empathy and see the flight from their own homeland as an expression of their feelings of despair and hopelessness.

We know from experience that things can go wrong if we let our actions be guided solely by emotions and immediate impulses. Therefore, we have learned, and are still learning, to self-regulate our emotions. But that doesn't mean putting a lid on them. Emotions are always more comprehensive than the thoughts; they are, so to speak, the surroundings in which thoughts arise. Local, spontaneous actions to welcome refugees and try to help them find something where they can use their own resources are examples that show that we have both knowledge, resources and enough reason to be able to treat other people, with their emotions, their knowledge and their reason, in a way that meets the others as people and not as problems.

There is no other way out of this than for there to be an ongoing conversation in society about how these challenges can be met in the best possible way. But there must be a conversation where both the rational and the non-rational in us are recognised.

Emmanuel Levinas puts it this way:

> "There are, if you will, tears that a state functionary (or functionary of any other socio-political order) does not see, and cannot see: the tears of the Other. In order for business to function well and run smoothly, it is absolutely necessary to affirm the infinite responsibility of everyone, and to everyone. In such a situation (of socio-political order), there is need of individual consciences, for only they can see violence, the violence flowing from the effective function of Reason itself. We must defend subjectivity against a certain disorder flowing from the Order of that universal Reason. In my view, the promotion and defense of subjectivity rests not on the fact that its egoism would be holy, but on the fact that only the ego can see the "secret tears" of the Other, tears brought about by the efficient function of the socio-political hierarchy. Consequently, subjectivity (of the responsibly established ego) is indispensable for the achievement of this non-violence which the state (and every socio-political order) seeks, but while also passing by the particularity of the ego and the Other." (Burggraeve 2002: 176–177).

As long as we stay within rational models of thought, theories will largely govern our actions. When we now expand the space and include both emotions and more inaccessible "unconscious memories" in our personality, theories will also recede more into the background. They will be able to support the thought where it is applied. At the same time, it is important to emphasize that thoughtlessness is not the only alternative to thinking. There is also an alternative on the other side of thinking: An alternative to just letting rational thinking rule is that thinking retains the connection with the deeper structures and processes in our minds.

A professional practice that is based exclusively on rules and instructions can just as easily be replaced by robots or fixed procedures. As Levinas emphasizes in the quotation above, only humans can see the violations and stresses that result from what he calls "The Order of universal Reason". The fact that a system is represented by people who can see "the Other's tears" is necessary not only to save the human, but for the system itself to be able to function (in that it is subject to constant improvement) and thus for society, which Levinas says in the quote above, should be able to achieve the care that every society seeks through its organization.

The biggest threat to a human society and a peaceful world is probably that so many of the smallest children do not receive the care that gives them the opportunity for the emotional interaction the brain needs to develop independent people, where the thoughts are still rooted deeper in the mind. In that case, the most important preventive work will be to give children a sufficiently good upbringing.

As a conclusion to this chapter, we will hear the story from a woman who, through her efforts, has shown that ethics is not something that comes in addition to professional work, but rather is a way of doing the work professionally.

Eva Joly: Our troublesome conscience

Eva Joly was born in 1943 as the daughter of a tailor and grew up as Gro Eva Farseth in Oslo, Norway. In 1964 she went to Paris as *au pair*. She married a Frenchman, studied law and in 1981 got a job as a lawyer with the French public prosecutors (Norby 2011). In the following years she made a rapid career in the French legal system.

During the 1990s, Eva Joly became a leading figure in the fight against economic crime. She added financial and technical resources to the investigative activities, and she used investigation methods that had not previously been used against economic crime – wiretapping, surveillance, seizures, detention, subpoenas, etc. She got powerful enemies. In the underground agitation against her, it was constantly alleged that she was driven by Protestant zeal. She was subjected to death threats and in recent years has had permanent bodyguards (Norby 2011).

In the book *Is This the World We Want?* (Joly 2005) she tells about how, as an interrogator in Paris, she helped to expose large-scale corruption in the oil company Elf. The investigation eventually pointed to people at the very top of the country's political leadership. In the introduction to her book, she writes:

> "By simply doing my job, I was threatened with death. I have been kept under the surveillance by rumour makers and the secret services, subjected to a pressure I would never have imagined possible: I was slandered and accused of the worst misdeeds. As if danger were on the side of justice. To get lost in the bottomless questions of why and how would not bring anything." (Joly 2003: 16)[15]

With her non-traditional background—and perhaps also as a woman in a male-dominated work environment—it is conceivable that Eva Joly could enter her work tasks with a greater range of human resources than the more limited rational ones that are often expected to form the basis for the exercise of a profession. It wasn't just her education as a lawyer that she took with her to work. She took the whole person with her, which meant she couldn't close her eyes to what she sensed was going on. She had sufficient courage to speak up, and she brought with her a strong sense of justice. Eva Joly has also shown the same in her later community involvement: being the voice "from the outside" who speaks out about what many others know, but about which they have been taught to remain silent.

Ethics was not a separate topic for Joly, something that came in addition to professional practice. The point for her was that what the rest of us call professional ethics, for her is part of being professional.

With her knowledge, experience and clear speech, Eva Joly has been widely used as a resource person by both authorities, business

---

15 Translated from the French edition by the present author.

and organisations. From 2009 to 2019 she was elected to the European Parliament as a representative of the party "The Greens".

Chapter 5:
Winding up

A short, preliminary summary

In this book I have explored the primacy of ethics by first asking what we may learn about this from professional helpers in a modern knowledge society. Their knowledge is managed today by the respective professions, a knowledge that is constantly supplied by new and valuable research, but which at the same time continues a practice based on human activities that have existed as long as humans themselves, and long before any theory and any stated ethics were shaped. In a knowledge-based society, this special position should give these professions a head start, ahead of the many professions that first arose with modern society. However, this head start can disappear if only the conscious and stated knowledge is considered valid. In this book, I have emphasized that this advance in knowledge has an ethical side, which we could call an ethical advantage. These original interpersonal activities are driven by an ethic that was there before the word "ethics" was even introduced. And it was there in all humans.

In chapter 1 we saw how the awareness of one's own self arises approximately in the middle of the second year of life in a dialogue with another person, usually the mother, in a context of goodness and as a continuation of the already established emotional communication. After that, we constantly practice the ability to shape thoughts alone. This means that even though rational thought models are presented as consistent and "self-sustaining", they are nevertheless formed in a continuous context with underlying and non-conscious processes. Consciousness was compared with a communication department whose task is to describe the will of the organism and the organization in a logically consistent manner and without internal contradictions, while the reality on the inside is not at all so logical. At the same time, we also saw how Freud, through his experience with patients, discovered that the subjective "from the inside" perspective is also necessary to understand what happens in the human mind.

Chapter 2 describes how Hans Skjervheim warned against getting carried away by "pure thinking", as he believed the postmodern philosophers in France in the 1970s and 1980s did. Most of us do like Skjervheim: We leave the most intricate and unrealistic philosophical logic when it loses its practical relevance. Skjervheim justified this by putting judgment over pure logic. If the consequences are too unreasonable, we will not join the line of thinking. In this book we have found an additional justification for doing the same: Recent knowledge tells us that a rational thought and action model in, for example, a workplace, rests on, or rather rests in, the narratives, the lifeworld and that which is prior to all memory and all recall.

Chapter 3 pointed to the difference between, on the one hand, "the pure and direct experience" we make as biological objects among objects, and on the other hand, the abstract and rational language of thought models, which are only like single points in a continuous physical reality. This helps us to understand how, in work with and for fellow human beings, we retrieve the communication we learned before we learned the abstract language, that is, the emotional and physical communication we learned as new-born. But we can also use language to get closer to that which is "prior to all memory and all recall", which is usually beyond the reach of our consciousness, for example in art or in inherited stories and myths. We also see examples of this in the health-related market. Alternative forms of treatment, medicines direct from nature and physical exercises to keep the body in shape are often linked to old and partly mythological stories, often from non-European cultures such as Chinese. They have survived because they are perceived to have a good effect, at the same time that rational medical science often cannot provide any explanation for this.

There are several thinkers who have tried to put into words experiences that rational thinking cannot describe. These thinkers also try to break away from how the established religions fill in where science falls short. In the previous chapter, we saw how Emmanuel Levinas describes ethics as something that arises in the subject's encounter with the Other. He does this by describing the subject's experience as an evocation of that which is "prior to all memory and all recall". He goes behind the subject's conscious experience of the encounter here and now. In this way, he transcends the philosophical method, phenomenology, from which he takes his point of departure. This is perhaps precisely why Levinas gives us descriptions of the encounter with the Other that many people recognize.

Spinoza revitalized

Another thinker who transcended both the recognized philosophical methods and the prevailing religious explanations was the Dutch philosopher Baruch Spinoza (1632–1677). Contrary to his older colleague, René Descartes (1596–1650), who with his renewal of philosophy had become the great authority of the time, Spinoza saw thinking and the material world as two sides of the same coin. And contrary to what all the prominent religions of his time preached, he called this totality of the world of thought and the material world "God" (Spinoza 1993).

Spinoza grew up in the Jewish community in Amsterdam. However, his early independent thinking provoked Jews as well as Christians and Cartesians. Among other things, he pointed out that while religious writings use figurative language, philosophy uses the language of reason. Therefore we find no philosophical truth in the religions (Eriksen 1994: 328). But the philosophical truths, as Descartes describes them, also have their limitations. Among other things, they do not take into account how important our emotions and our intuition are in order to gain knowledge about the world that we cannot stand outside and observe, because it is a whole of which we ourselves are a part, both materially and mentally.

With the knowledge we have today about the brain and its development, we know that thinking activity is part of the neurobiological processes, and we know that emotions play together with thinking as a basis for what we say and do. This was also Spinoza's point 350 years ago. Therefore, it will be interesting to look more closely at what else this thinker said, in the light of all the knowledge that has come to be after his time.

As Spinoza saw it, the material world and the world of thought are two different expressions of the same whole. With what we know today, we could say that this is something we get confirmed when we experience intersubjectivity, that is to say that we can share common experiences from the same lifeworld with others, so that to a certain extent we have a common world of thought. But not only that: Humans who have nothing else in common other than the fact that they are humans, develop in the biological body and in the emotional interaction with first their mother and later with others, a world of thought in their first years of life that characterizes the common human: an ability to empathize and eventually an ability to think and to acquire knowledge.

In his book *Ethics* (Spinoza 1993), Spinoza sets out a number of theses which he then assembles into a comprehensive and consistent system of thought, written in Latin as a mathematical treatise according to the scientific ideals of the time. Here he begins with an assumption based on an observation that everything in the world, both living and dead matter, is characterized by a will to continue being what it is (in Latin: *conatus essendi*): "Each thing in so far as it is in itself endeavours to persist in its own being." (Spinoza 1993: 89). It is this drive for self-preservation that drives us humans. We are therefore not driven by goals that we have set ourselves. What we humans call goals is more situational and can be defined as what the individual, possibly several together, seems to be striving towards at all times in order to maintain themselves.

Human reason is our most important aid to sustaining ourselves. It is with the help of reason that we can survive, both with body and with mind. But emotions also play an important role here. They can be either a support or a hindrance in our attempts to sustain ourselves. Emotions cannot replace reason, but they can be an important addition to it, as long as reason understands emotions as what they are, namely as emotions.

For Spinoza there are two kinds of emotions: positive and negative. He defines the positive emotions as joy or emotions associated with joy, and the negative he defines as pain or emotions associated with pain. All positive emotions strengthen the faculties of reason in the human endeavour, all negative emotions weaken it. This happens in practice by positive emotions being expressed through play and pleasurable activities, while the negative emotions are expressed through duty and non-pleasurable activities. Since the negative emotions are obstacles to maintaining ourselves, it is important to regulate these with reason. Negative emotions should not be repressed or fought, because they can tell us when, for example, there is a danger that threatens. But they must mobilize reason to find out how the situation can be handled, instead of letting the negative emotions have a free outlet in actions that destroy others and thus also themselves, since we are parts of the same whole.

What also characterizes Spinoza is that he does not see ethics as a field of its own, that is, separate from our knowledge of what is. The distinction between what is and what should be is an artificial distinction that can lead astray, because morality then stands outside the real world. Ethics—what we should do, and what we think about it—follows naturally from how we understand the world and our place in it. His *conatus essendi* (see above) is not a normative statement, it is an observation. But given this observation, Spinoza says that since it is now the case that everything belongs together in the same whole, it is not reasonable, that is, it does not contribute to my own self-preservation, to oppose others (unless it has to be done for the sake of the whole). Conflicts are partly due to insufficient knowledge, partly because we are ruled by emotions. What serves my self-preservation best is what also serves others. There is always something bigger than a conflict. Good actions are therefore not something I choose to "do penance" or to sacrifice myself for others. It's something I choose because, ultimately, it's in my best interest. This is perhaps precisely what Ibsen wants to tell us about Terje Vigen (see page 58), who chose not to take revenge on the English lord. As with all poetry, it is on the way from the poet to the reader that the ambiguous interpretation arises, and the Terje Vigen poem can in any case be interpreted so that Terje's deed was not carried out based on any kind of idea of charity, forgiveness or mercy, but rather for himself to become a better person, that is, to become a part of the I that he had lost in the tragedy many years before.

Spinoza says of knowledge that it can have three sources:

- intuition, which is an immediate experience of connections in the whole

- systematic science, and

- individuals' assumptions

According to Spinoza, only the last of these sources can be the cause of error. Here he differs from, among others, Descartes by claiming that intuition, as an immediate experience of the whole, is also a source of knowledge.[16] But he agrees with Descartes that individuals' assumptions can be wrong if they are not tested through a systematic science.

---

16 Here I would like to recall what was said in chapter 1 (p. 14) about intuitive caring practice.

Since we humans are governed to such a large extent by emotions—and by insufficient knowledge—we need an authority, for example a state, which can prevent us from destroying each other and thus ourselves. The state's means of preventing this is to make use of the fact that we are governed by emotions, including fear. That is to say, we are prevented from destroying others because we fear the punishment that comes with it. The laws are based on reason, but the laws themselves do not make us reasonable people, says Spinoza.

As an individual, I can do whatever I want, but random choices do not give me a sense of freedom. I get a feeling of freedom instead when, in my pursuit of my own self-preservation, I act in accordance with the whole of which I am a part. To do that, I must have both knowledge of this whole and positive emotions about it, which I also know are emotions. This, says Spinoza, is the way to the good life.

For Spinoza, there are two kinds of knowledge about the whole: knowledge about concrete events and objects in time and space and more generally valid knowledge that is independent of time and space. Both forms of knowledge are true, but only the latter can give us freedom, that is, what we need to manage our lives. Here it may be difficult for us modern people to understand what Spinoza means, but we can imagine that the first type of knowledge is what we usually call knowledge, and which is developed through the sciences. The second type of knowledge is more intuitive. We can imagine that it is the experience we can have by being in nature and experiencing ourselves as part of it, and perhaps also in the world of thought, by entering a text, whether it is scientific or fictional (or religious), which can call forth in us something that we recognise. This is therefore not what we today call knowledge, but rather what Husserl called "pure and immediate experience" by being in the world of life "as objects among other objects" (page 41). This knowledge is not acquired with the help of a systematic method and observation of the surroundings, but by understanding oneself as part of something bigger. Spinoza called this a knowledge "to conceive the essence of the body under a species of eternity" (*sub specie aeternitatis*) (p. 210). He thus gave it a character of infinity. In chapter 3 I described how physical and biological reality has such a form of continuous infinity, in contrast to what we call knowledge, which corresponds to Spinoza's knowledge of concrete events in time and space, and which has a smaller scope because this knowledge can be numbered.

Spinoza thus claimed that the material world and the world of thought are not two separate worlds. Here, as mentioned, he disagreed with Descartes, who built his entire theory on this distinction. Therefore, Descartes did not come into conflict with the leaders of the religious institutions, what Spinoza did to a great extent. Moreover, Descartes' distinction between ideas and matter proved to be very useful for the further development of science, at least the natural sciences and at least until today. This is probably because the I-subject, with its world of thought, can stand outside the material world and describe its laws, which enable us to use nature to reach our purposes. The problem arises when we discover that we ourselves are part of this nature, and that we are even completely at its mercy. Spinoza can help us here. The thinking is something that is contained in the material world. The thinking and conscious subject arises and develops in a body, as part of an objectively given material reality.

For Spinoza, we humans strive to maintain ourselves as parts of something bigger and more, and what gives a good life is to act in accordance with what is best for this whole. But it therefore requires having both knowledge of this whole and positive emotions about it. A limited, rational system of thinking and acting in which the world is viewed from an outside position is not enough. Stated with the knowledge we possess today, it means that in order to have a good life, we as ego-subjects must enter into the whole of which we are a part, and not keep out the underlying processes such as the emotions and other neurobiological processes that can touch our consciousness from a past "prior to all memory and all recall".

What makes work meaningful?

What is meaningful work? Here we must be careful not to lose ourselves in "pure thinking", as Skjervheim warned us against (see page 28). The discussion should be linked to our everyday reality. Fortunately, it is not difficult as long as we are talking about professional help. The very fact that we are here faced with basic human activities that have been there as long as there have been humans, aligns with the experiences that these activities make meaning in themselves in the meeting with those in need and in meeting their needs. This is not as obvious for professions that arose with a more modern industrial society and later in a society where more and more people make a living by selling various services in a market. In the beginning of this book, I suggested that the helping professions derive their motivation, their knowledge and their ethics from something deeper in us than the professional knowledge that have come about later. It is also my experience that the professional helpers we are talking about here find the work in itself meaningful. In any case, it applies to the part of their work that involves the primary activity, which is helping and providing care.

What we see, on the other hand, as a disturbing factor in the practice of these professions today is that more and more of their working time is spent on other, indirect activities, such as reporting, form filling and coordination, and that the work requirements and the pace are simultaneously sharpened so much that the professional helpers are forced to do a worse job than what they think is reasonable, due to time pressure. When managers impose such non-professional tasks on their employees or press them for time, they simultaneously take away from the organization its most important source of energy, namely the professionals' motivation, job satisfaction and experience of doing something meaningful. This energy is not recorded in any budget, accounting or planning documents, because it is beyond the reach of the conscious and rational knowledge of management, finance and organization. But when, due to strong work pressure and a lot of side work, it is lost, the result will still be felt on the accounts and on the quality of the services.

One side of Spinoza's contribution that is well recognized throughout working life is the strengthening of the workings of reason that positive emotions contribute to, for example how much better a job is done when it is driven by a joy of work. But job satisfaction is not something that can be decided. The positive reinforcement between reason and emotions rather means that when rational work is facilitated by the fact that it is also pleasurable, it can be a sign that what is being done is also for the good of something more than just the explicitly stated, rational purpose.

Those who lead organizations that carry out these activities are thus fortunate that they do not need to motivate their employees or help them find meaning in their work. The motivation and meaning lie in the work tasks themselves. What they must be careful of, however, is not to impose on their employees what deprives them of this motivation, meaning and joy. These driving forces are, as already mentioned, the organisation's most important source of energy. The managers' tasks must be to release and manage this energy in the best possible way. But it is not currently clear how this can be done. Managing the rational thinking and action systems, such as budgets, work and action plans, is far simpler, because it only requires the part of the human potential that involves rational thinking, and which can thus be done outside the lifeworld where the services are performed.

It is my hope that this book can also help managers to release the energy that lies in their employees' motivation and job satisfaction, so that they get this through the meaning that the work itself gives. What can politicians and managers do to get a good health and social service, good kindergartens, good schools and other good working places where any kind of service is given? A good start is to ask the employees who meet daily those who receive help and service. This is also done in many places through attempts to invite the employees into strategy discussions. But that is not enough, because then you have already limited yourself to the framework set by the language. It would be more radical if the leaders themselves entered the everyday reality where care and service is given, and thus also familiarize themselves with the world of thought that is part of this lifeworld.

Earlier in this book, we have seen that in all people—assuming good enough care and emotional communication in the first years of life—an ability to empathize with other people is embodied. Newer knowledge in neurobiology can also tell us that such an ability is a prerequisite for later learning, of language, abstract symbols and eventually specialist knowledge. But we have also seen that the knowledge which I previously (in chapter 3) called countable, can never replace the pure and immediate experience of being an object among objects in the lifeworld, which, in contrast to the world of thoughts, is a physical and biological continuum. Rather, it is the case that knowledge follows from experience, that it will always have to do so, but that it will never be able to replace it. Precisely for this reason, we humans constantly try to exceed the actual knowledge we can acquire about the world. We try to transcend the limitations of rational language in our own ways. For some, religious language makes sense. For others, other narratives or different motivational settings can complement the understanding. These are not competing forms of understanding, as long as they are recognized as precisely subjective forms of understanding. In all cases, it is about finding a connection between the world outside us and something inside ourselves that will never be able to be brought fully into consciousness, which gives us an experience of being part of a larger connection, experienced purely and directly, before any theories about it are made.

One of the things that strikes us the most when we read Spinoza today, and especially seen against the background of the new knowledge that helps to revitalize him, is that he goes in the opposite direction of a trend that is very prevalent in our society: the encouragement to individual self-assertion, of being an *I for myself*. When we also include the growing recognition that a society with a political and an economic system that is fundamentally driven by such self-assertion has become a direct threat to the climate and environment and to a more just and peaceful world, Spinoza only becomes even more relevant than ever, almost 350 years after he wrote his book.[17]

Unfortunately, Spinoza's thoughts come up against some obstacles in the economic and political power structures. It has become attractive, both in terms of finances and social status, to move up in the hierarchies. Then you can avoid the strenuous work and, in addition, be given, or give yourself, a better pay. Perhaps there is an opportunity in a new technology where machines can do more and more of the (countable) things that machines can do, so that what is left for humans is what machines will not be able to do, because it presupposes being part of the biological and continuous reality. In nursing, caring, training, service providing and other helping professions, it is important to find a good division of labour between man and machine that makes human work even more meaningful. This could change the content of the work both for those who meet help on a daily basis, and for their managers. For everyone, it will be their qualities as humans that will be the most important. Such a development may also increase the possibilities of giving the actual professionals greater economic and political power: They can no longer be replaced by machines, while after all it is they, and not their managers, who have the core experience.

Some will probably think this is too optimistic. It probably is, too, if it is only read as a prediction of the future. But perhaps not if it is read as a description of a space of opportunity, a space of opportunity that needs its brave and dedicated women and men to be used.

"To be nothing"

Music is a form of expression where body, emotions and thoughts meet. Mastering an instrument (including the voice) requires a lot

---

17 See, however, the conclusion following this chapter for a further and modifying discussion of this problem.

of awareness both of the body and of technique. At the same time, playing an instrument—the voice included—will require an ability to retrieve the life that takes place behind the thoughts. With its narrative, but at the same time wordless, form, music often hits something in us that lies in the body from our very earliest years of life, yes, even from before birth. Another characteristic of live music as an art form is that it only exists there and then, in time and space, and is gone when the last note is played. It gives music a special place in the lifeworld.

Folk music has more and deeper roots in that which is "prior to all memory and all recall". It is also striking how folk music performers from different parts of the world can communicate with each other just by playing, without words. We can see this when performers from different cultures find each other in the genre called "world music".

In Chapter 2, we saw how Svetlana Alexievich portrays war as women do it, where "there are no heroes and incredible victories, but simply people who are busy doing inhumanly human things " (page 36). Also in music, and especially folk music, highlighting heroes and "incredible victories" is unimportant. At least it's not typically female. In the book *To be nothing* by Benedicte Maurseth (2014) we read about the author's meetings and conversations with her teacher, fiddler Knut Hamre, and his stories about his teachers and other folk musicians. Folk music is in a special position because it is handed down from one generation to the next directly and not in written form. The handover takes place in a (continuous) reality and not via (countable) notes. In these traditions, there must always be a balance between being faithful to tradition and putting one's own signature on the music as a performer, which is also important for the music to live and reach those who listen, and create recognition with something they didn't know lay there.

Knut Hamre is one of Norway's foremost folk music performers. But as Maurseth portrays him, he has no sense of competition or other ways of highlighting himself. In the book we can read the following:

"There is something at the bottom of Knut's heart that inclines towards the religious, but he no longer finds the same in the church room as when he was a child, as there is a lot of church history that is too jarring. But the belief in the spiritual power is still as strong.

KH: Now I feel more drawn to the way the Quakers think, that there is a light in us, that there is a bit of God in and around us all. I also like the fact that they don't engage in preaching.

BM: *I have heard you say many times that you are "nothing"?*

KH: By that I mean that it is not me who plays, although it is quite obvious that I am the physical player. There is something else playing through me.

BM: *But you as a person must be important so that what is really important has a channel to come through?*

KH: The person, that is the personal Knut Hamre, is not important. It's never about me, but about the art, which is much bigger than me. Therefore I am nothing.

BM: *Which is the same as a medium?*

KH: The word medium has various associations, and there are many prejudices linked to it. Therefore, I use it as little as possible and replace it with nothing. The idea that one is a medium for something other than oneself can be difficult to decide whether one only believes in the individual. But if you see yourself as part of a larger context, it can make sense and security to think like this" (Maurseth 2014:140–141)[18].

---

18 Translated from Norwegian by the present author.

The statement "I am nothing" is particularly thought-provoking precisely because it is said by someone who many would characterize as one of our most outstanding music performers and cultural bearers. It is therefore not about being nothing as others see it, but about seeing oneself as insignificant within the whole in which one participates through one's own efforts. At the same time, it also points to an indisputable truth in the light of Spinoza's *sub specie aeternitatis* (pages 79–80): A single human life counts for nothing "under a species of eternity". As individuals, we are all parts of a larger whole. When we gradually "zoom out" in the objectively given material world of life, both in time and in space, we disappear more and more towards "nothingness".

The women's stories

In this book, I have presented five women at the end of each of the five chapters. Each of these women's stories is either a supplement or a corrective to, or they enter into a dialogue with, what has been presented earlier in the chapter. What they all have in common is that they have a story to tell. One of the reasons for these presentations is that stories are the beginning of new knowledge. We can say that a story is the first account, from what Husserl called "plain certainty of experience" from the lifeworld (see page 42), the everyday reality in which we all live and make our experiences, as objects among other objects, before we as ego-subjects are "experiencing it, contemplating it, valuing it, related to it purposefully…". All the chapters thus end with something that can be the beginning of a new knowledge.

Siri Hustvedt's "story of my nerves" expands neurobiological and psychological knowledge by pointing out its limitations. The scientific knowledge of my inner mind cannot answer all questions. It is part of life that there is something we just have to live with, and that by putting ourselves outside in an attempt to understand the world, we also put ourselves outside both ourselves and life.

The stories of Svetlana Alexievich about women in war bring

to life their pure and immediate experiences. These are not the stories of historians, politicians or military strategists. She received the Nobel Prize in Literature for her stories because, despite the limitations inherent in the words, she is able to open the reader's eyes to the fact that what usually remains as "the story of the war" will always be something other than the war itself as it is experienced, directly and immediately.

Edith Stein's story is the story of her own life, as she has partly told it herself. With her brilliant intelligence, she came at a young age into the group of the then greatest philosopher in our part of the world, Edmund Husserl. She renewed his phenomenological method, but as a woman she did not receive the recognition for what men (including Husserl himself) later received for similar thoughts. She came to the conclusion that then it could be the same; she found in religion the necessary extension of the scientific thinking she sought, and through it she found a meaning in what we might call everyday reality.

Eva Joly talks about her life as a corruption hunter at the public prosecutor's office in France. Her story shows that ethics is something real and not something theoretical. Her help with how to proceed when she discovers that something wrong has been done, she does not get from fully formulated and adopted "ethical guidelines", but instead from the immediate sense of justice that is embedded in all of us, as something wordless that is laid down in us once, and which we can retrieve because it lies there as what Levinas calls a memory from "prior to all memory and all recall ", or, as Løgstrup calls it, as a supreme expression of life which "sets the situation in motion" and where the person "must constantly play himself into it" (page 63).

Finally, Benedicte Maurseth talks about her teacher, Knut Hamre, who by playing a folk music instrument creates a pure and immediate experience that brings a wordless musical tradition on to the next generation, as he himself has had it handed down from the generation before him. Music is part of the lifeworld that everyone can be in, as objects among other objects, but which we relate to as I-subjects, either as a performer, as a listener, as a commentator or as a professional. The art of the exercise is to be a subject and an object at the same time. Through her questions and observations and with her prerequisites to know what this is all about, because she shares the fiddler's lifeworld, Benedicte Maurseth manages to tell us readers how one of our great performers has become great for others in his time by being small, by being nothing, to himself.

Concluding remarks on business, ethics and the future

In the introduction to this book the idea was launched that a business life driven by the self-interest of individuals can nevertheless be liveable simply because it is populated by humans, who are more than rational decision-makers – and more than algorithm-controlled machines. How can what is written above shed more light on this idea?

As the title of this book indicates, ethics take precedence in our lives: We come into the world surrounded by care. In order for our consciousness to emerge, there must be other persons who help us, with their unconditional care, also called love. Eventually language emerges, and the always lacking quantity of available words is compensated for by a mutual willingness and efforts to understand each other.

Later we experience that we cannot believe everything that is said or written. But since we have first learned to trust the words of others, we often make the same mistake over and over again, namely trusting what we hear or read. Gradually, we learn that untrue language can serve a purpose: For example, when a business, either through its name or public statements, expresses openness and social responsibility, while under the cover of these presentations it continues with the exact opposite.[19]

When we are never completely at the mercy of what is said verbally and its source, it is because we have developed an ability to place what is said or written in a context. This applies especially when we are in the same physical reality, because a communication there becomes infinitely richer than just the words used. In addition, through experience, we have developed a judgment to be able to evaluate what we have heard or read.

It is easy to criticize—and moralise over—the business world because it is driven by the self-interest of the individual actors. Against this self-interest, an ethic has traditionally been set up that has its source outside the self-centred business. Such a move fits well into a tradition where ethics is presented as a counterpart to the egocentric drive of individuals. To Levinas, this source is the other person's face, which is beyond the subject's control and even comprehension (see page 64).[20] In religions, the source of ethics is some form of deity that primarily exists outside the human self.

A weakness following the assumption that the source of ethics is external is that ethics is then regarded as a subject in itself, and thus viewed as an addition to professional knowledge and practice, rather than being an integrated part of these. One has to go elsewhere, to some appointed ethical authority, to some existing guidelines, or to a separate ethical discourse to find answers to what is right and wrong in a given situation. In this way, ethics can easily become too theoretical and thus create a distance from professional as well as everyday life.

This book points to an alternative to such an external source of ethics. As we have seen, new knowledge about the development of the brain tells us that the I-subject emerges in the infant gradually within a context of goodness in an interaction with a caregiver. We have seen how language and thoughts are connected with emotions and intuition in a larger, organic context, also in relationships

---

19 This paradox is described and discussed in more depth in Aasland (2009).
20 When it comes to ethics in business, this is elaborated further in Aasland (2004) and (2022).

with others. This knowledge therefore challenges how we usually understand ethics: ethics does not first come from the outside, from an alterity to the self. Instead, it develops from a potential in the body given through evolution and then realised through interaction with first a primary caregiver, then other persons in the immediate surroundings. This knowledge indicates that we should consider the origin of ethics as interpersonal rather than external.

In addition, this knowledge challenges several of the dichotomies we usually take for granted when we orientate ourselves in the world: the distinction between body and mind, between the objective and the subjective, between reason and emotion and between facts and values.

We have seen how Spinoza based his *Ethics* on an observation that everything in the world seems to have a will to continue being what they are. In our efforts to continue being who we are, we humans use our reason, aided by both emotions and intuition. We seek knowledge of the whole of which we are a part, and we understand that helping our surroundings to continue to be who they are also helps ourselves in our efforts to continue to be who we are. (With some help from a state authority, preventing us from being governed by our emotions).

For Spinoza, the knowledge of what we should do is inseparable from our knowledge of what there is. To do the right thing is to do what is in accordance with our own self-preservation, as long as one applies the best available knowledge of our place in a larger whole, supported by our emotions and our intuition.

The world today faces some serious threats on climate and biodiversity, migration and a growing inequality. A new ethic is beginning to emerge from below: more and more people are becoming concerned and asking themselves what they can do. How can we act in a way that takes care of nature, the planet and all its species? In this situation a Spinozean approach may seem more suitable than the notion of an ethics that has its source outside our own lifeworld.

A Spinozean approach will require a greater humility in the use of nature and its resources. As we know, climate change is due to the tapping of fossil energy carried out in the belief that nature exists for humans to exploit. The same applies to nature interventions that reduce the diversity of species.

What will be the role of business in such an approach? Instead of proceeding theoretically, we can go back to the lifeworld, where people, also in business, participate with more than their ability to think rationally. Both employers and employees enter the business with their whole selves. They may have a gut feeling that what their business is doing is not good for the whole. They can also enter with their ability to use their intuition and be creative to find new products and services, or to produce the same products and services in ways that do not destroy the whole.

This book began by asking what we can learn from professional help to understand how ethics works in society, because in these professions there is an underlying ethic to serve others than oneself. With today's global crises, ethics are beginning to seep into other professions as well, including those in business and industry. Fortunately, the business world has a place to go and learn: the professions that have always been aimed at helping others than themselves. It is not just the sick, the elderly and children who must be cared for. It is the planet, it's nature, all living species, including the people who suffer as a result of the changes in climate and nature, and as a result of migration and poverty. This critical situation changes the criteria for what constitutes relevant knowledge and it changes the way businesses are managed, among other things by bringing out the motivation, the energy and the ethics that are inherent in the employees. When this is in fact a realistic scenario it is because ultimately it is about pursuing one's self-interest, as business always has done, only with the addition that decisions must be based on a knowledge of the whole of which we are all a part, so that taking care of the whole is also taking care of oneself.

To base our lives and decisions on the knowledge that our

thoughts and emotions are only a small part of large and unknown biological processes, and recognizing that we humans are only a small part of a larger whole that it is in our own interest to take care of, is an approach that is compatible with what is meant by a sustainable development. This applies to professional help, it applies to business, and it applies to us all.

Literature

Aarnes, Asbjørn (1993). Emmanuel Levinas – liv og verk. In Levinas, E. *Den Annens humanisme* (203–228). Oslo: Aschehoug.

Aasland, Dag G. (2004). "On the Ethics Behind "Business Ethics"". Journal of Business Ethics 53: 3 – 8

Aasland, Dag G. (2009). *Ethics and Economy: After Levinas.* London: MayFly Books

Aasland, Dag G. (2017). *Frå mål til mening: Ord og virkelighet i profesjonell hjelp.* Oslo: Gyldendal Akademisk

Aasland, Dag G. (2022). "Re-humanizing Business: Some Lessons from Levinas and Their Implications". In Dion, M. *et al* (ed.) *Humanizing Business: What Humanities Can Say to Business.* Cham, Switzerland: Springer Nature.

Alexievich, Svetlana (2017). *The Unwomanly Face of War: an Oral History of Women in World War II.* London: Penguin Random House

Barlow, Horace B. (1980). Nature's Joke: A Conjecture on the Biological Role of Consciousness. I: Josephson, B.D. og V.S. Ramachandrand, V.S. (red.). *Consciousness and the Physical Worlds* (81–90). Oxford: Pergamon Press.

Burggraeve, Roger (2002). *The Wisdom of Love in the Service of Love: Emmanuel Levinas on Justice, Peace, and Human Rights.* Milwaukee, WI: Marquette University Press.

Burggraeve, Roger (2008). Affected by the Face of the Other. The Levinasian Movement from the Exteriority to the Interiority of the Infinite. I: Kajon, I., Baccarini, E., Brezzi, F. og Hansel, J. (red.). *Emmanuel Levinas. Prophetic Inspiration and Philosophy.* Roma: Atti del Convegno internaionale per il Centario delle nascita, Rome May 24–27 2006.

Enders, Giulia (2014). *Darm mit Charme: Alles uber ein unterschätstes Organ.* Berlin: Ullstein. English translation: *Gut: The Inside Story of Our Body's Most Underrated Organ.* Vancouver/Berkley: Greystone Books (2015).

Eriksen, Trond Berg (1994). *Undringens labyrinter. Forelesninger over filosofiens historie.* Oslo: Universitetsforlaget.

Figueiredo, Ivo de (2006). *Henrik Ibsen. Mennesket.* Oslo: Aschehoug.

Fonagy, Peter (2006). Udvikling af psykopatologi fra tidlig barndom til voksenliv. Den mystiske udfoldelse av forstyrrelser over tid. InFonagy, P., Schore, A.N., Stern, D.N. og Sørensen, J.H. *Affektregulering i udvikling og psykoterapi.* Copenhagen: Hans Reitzels Forlag.

Freud, Sigmund (1957). The unconscious. *The Standard Edition of the Complete Psychological Works of Sigmund Freud*, bind XIV (166–215). London: The Hogarth Press.

Freud, Sigmund (1961). The Ego and the Id. *The Standard Edition of the Complete Psychological Works of Sigmund Freud*, volume XIX (3-66). London: The Hogarth Press.

Freud, Sigmund (1966). Project for a Scientific Psychology. (Bearbeidet og første gang publisert i 1950). *The Standard Edition of the Complete Psychological Works of Sigmund Freud*, bind I. London: The Hogarth Press.

Husserl, Edmund (1970). *The Crisis of European Sciences and Transcendental Phenomenology*. Evanston, Ill.: Northwestern University Press.

Hustvedt, Siri (2009). *The Shaking Woman or a History of My Nerves*. New York: Henry Holt and Company.

Joly, Eva and Laurent Beccaria (2003). *Est-ce dans ce monde-là que nous voulons vivre?* Paris: Les Arènes. English translation: *Is This the World We Want?* Citizen Press (2005).

Knausgård, Karl Ove (2018). *Spring*. Translated from the Norwegian by Ingvild Burkey. London: Penguin Random House.

Levinas, Emmanuel (1991). *Otherwise than Being or Beyond Essence*. Dordrecht: Kluwer Academic Publishers.

Levinas, Emmanuel (2003). *Humanism of the Other*. Chicago: University of Illinois.

Lewis, Michael (2014). *The Rise of Consciousness and the Development of Emotional Life*. New York/London: The Guilford Press.

Løgstrup, Knud E. (2013). *Opgør med Kierkegaard*. Aarhus: Forlaget Klim

Matthis, Irène (2014). Freud i 2000-talet: Neuropsykoanalysen och det subjektiva perspektivet. *Agora* 01–02/2014: 269–291. Oslo: Aschehoug.

Maurseth, Benedicte (2014). *Å vera ingenting. Samtalar med spelemannen Knut Hamre*. Oslo: Samlaget.

Nelson, Katherine (1996). *Language in Cognitive Development. Emergence of the Mediated Mind*. Cambridge: Cambridge University Press.

Norby, Reginald (2011, 9. desember). Eva Joly. In *Norsk biografisk leksikon*. Downloaded 29 januar 2016 from https://nbl.snl.no/Eva_Joly.

Posselt, Teresia Renata (2005). *Edith Stein. The Life of a Philosopher and Carmelite*. Washington DC: ICS Publications.

Schore, Allan N. (1994). *Affect Regulation and the Origin of the Self. The Neurobiology of Emotional Development.* Hillsdale, NJ: Lawrence Erlbaum Associates.

Schore, Allan N. (2001). "Effects of a secure attachment relationship on right brain development, affect regulation, and mental health." *Infant Mental Health Journal,* 22 (1–2): 7–66.

Schore, Allan N. (2002). "Advances in Neuropsychoanalusis, Attachment Theory, and Trauma Research: Implications for Self Psychology." In Joseph Lichtenberg (ed.) *Psychonalytical Inquiry,* Vol 22/3, Tha Analytic Press (433-485).

Schore, Allan N. (2006). "Landvindinger i neuropsykoanalyse, tilknytningsteori og traumeforskning. Implikationer for selvpsykologien." I: Fonagy mfl. *Affektregulering i udvikling og psykoterapi.* København: Hans Reitzels Forlag.

Skjervheim, Hans (1959). *Objektivismen og studiet av mennesket.* Oslo: Gyldendal.

Skjervheim, Hans (1992). Invitasjon til (kulturelt(?) sjølvmord?. I: Skjervheim, H. *Filosofi og dømmekraft* (s. 45–58). Oslo: Universitetsforlaget.

Smith, Lars (2014). Foreldres intuitive omsorgsatferd. *Scandinavian Psychologist,* 1, e1. http://dx.doi.org/10.15714/scandpsychol.1.e1

Spinoza, Baruch (1993). *Ethics and Treatise on the Correction of the Intellect.* Rutland, Vermont: Everyman.

Stein, Edith (1989). *On the Problem of Empathy.* Washington DC: ICS publications.

Strachey, James (1966). *The Standard Edition of the Complete Psychological Works of Sigmund Freud,* bind I. London: The Hogart Press.

Sørbø, Jan Inge (2002). *Hans Skjervheim – ein intellektuell biografi.* Oslo: Samlaget.

Tustin, F. (1981). Psychological birth and psychological catastrophe (181–196). In Grotstein, J. (red.). *Do I Dare Disturb the Universe.* London: Karnac.

Winnicott, David W. (1990a). The theory of the parent-infant relationship. I: *The Maturational Processes and the Facilitating Environment* (37–55). London: Karnac Books og The Institute of Psycho-Analysis.

Winnicott, David W. (1990b), «Ego Distortion in Terms of True and False Self". In *The Maturational Processes and the Facilitating Environment* (140–152). London: Karnac Books og The Institute of Psycho-Analysis.

Øverland, Janneken (2015, 29. september). Siri Hustvedt. I: *Store norske leksikon.* Downloaded January 28 2016 fr https://snl.no/Siri_Hustvedt.

Milton Keynes UK
Ingram Content Group UK Ltd.
UKHW021031260224
438483UK00007BB/105